HOW TO BUILD CONFIDENCE IN YOUR CHILD

How to Build Confidence in Your Child

Dr James Dobson

Hodder & Stoughton
LONDON   SYDNEY   AUCKLAND

Copyright © 1974, 1979 by Fleming H. Revell Co.

First published in Great Britain in 1982 as *Hide or Seek*
This edition 1997

10 9 8 7 6 5 4 3 2 1

British Library Cataloguing in Publication Data
A record for this book is available from the British Library

ISBN 0 340 69413 0

Offset by Avon Dataset Ltd, Bidford-on-Avon, Warks
Printed and bound in Great Britain by
Cox & Wyman, Reading, Berks

Hodder and Stoughton
A division of Hodder Headline PLC
338 Euston Road
London NW1 3BH

This book is dedicated in deepest respect to my father, whose influence on my life has been profound. I watched him closely throughout my childhood, yet he never disappointed me. Not once did I see him compromise his inner convictions and personal ethics. Thus, his values became my values and his life has charted the path for my own. Now it is my task, in turn, to be found worthy of the two little ones who call me 'Dad'.

Contents

Preface To The Revised Edition

How to Build Confidence in Your Child was written five years ago as an expression of my deep concern for the children of the world. Since that time, more than 252,000 copies have been sold in America and numerous foreign countries. It has been translated into German, Chinese, Spanish, Portuguese, and Hebrew. Thus, I suppose it is now appropriate to reveal the humbling story of how this manuscript came to be written, and why it almost landed in the trash can.

My first book was entitled *Dare to Discipline*, and was written with ease in a matter of five months. Thus, I was very confident, as I sat down to prepare my second book – the one you are now reading. But God had some lessons to teach me about self-sufficiency and independence.

I will never forget taking the first sixty pages with me to visit my parents in Kansas City. My father has always been my silent partner in projects of this nature. His judgment as a tough but loving critic has been priceless to me. That's why I asked him to read the first chapters, just minutes after my arrival at my parents' home.

Dad began reading the manuscript while I watched his expression for clues that would reveal his thoughts. After turning pages silently for twenty minutes, he did something that devastated me: he *yawned*! Believe me, it was no sleepy yawn. His was unmistakably a *bored* yawn. That wordless assessment hit me like a blow from a hammer, even though he followed it with several polite comments, such as, 'That's fine,' and 'I think you're on the right track.' My dad had no dishonest bones in his body, and even though he was trying to be encouraging, he could not sound convincing. The enthusiasm he had shown for every page of *Dare to Discipline* was simply not there.

I packed the manuscript in my briefcase several days later and went home. Every time I would think about working on the project, I could see my dad yawning. Finally mustering all the self-discipline at my command, I began writing again. But the pages came slowly and required much effort. I have always had a certain verbal flair, but it failed me at this moment of truth. By sheer determination, I wrote another sixty pages before grinding to a halt once more.

Pressing hospital and university responsibilities kept me from concentrating on the project for several months, leading my wife, Shirley, and me to plan a 'working' vacation devoted to my book. We selected the Sheraton Hotel in Waikiki Beach, Honolulu, hoping to be inspired by the beauty of that island paradise. It was a wise choice. Within a week, the book was virtually finished.

I gave a handwritten copy to Shirley, whose views I have also learned to trust. She left the room and returned three hours later with a grim face.

'I can't explain it, Jim,' she said. 'Something is not right. It just doesn't hang together.'

'Yeah, I know,' I said.

Having been successful in virtually everything I had tried to accomplish, I was unprepared for this brush with failure. Dad's yawn seemed to rise before me in mockery and disdain.

Finally I turned to Shirley and said, 'I know the message of this book is needed by parents and their children. They are hurting, and I can help. But maybe God doesn't want me to write it for some reason.'

'Then what do you intend to do?' she asked.

'I'm going to spend *one* more day on this book. Only *one*! I plan to attack the entire manuscript with a pair of scissors tomorrow morning. Nothing I've written will be safe from deletion or rearrangement. I also plan to fast tomorrow going without food in an atmosphere of prayer and dependence on God]. Then if I still feel defeated by tomorrow night, I will throw away what I've written and go home.'

With that we went to bed. The next morning Shirley and I began our day with a fervent prayer for God's guidance and blessing. She departed for a shopping trip, and I tore into my manuscript. Seven hours later, *How to Build Confidence in Your Child* emerged in much the same form that you see it today. Every piece fell together like a jigsaw puzzle, as though the Great Designer were guiding my efforts. And although I have written several other books that have sold over a million copies, *How to Build Confidence in Your Child* remains my favourite to this moment.

It is now obvious that God permitted me to go through that period of self-doubt for a purpose. Nothing similar has happened before or since. You see, I had begun to depend on myself, instead of being an instrument of His purpose and plan. I believe He wanted me to understand that my 'ministry' to families is not my own, but is managed by His own hand. I responded by giving my meagre talent back to the Source whence it came originally.

Oh, yes, and about my father! He read the entire manuscript in one sitting without (to my knowledge) a single yawn. In fact, he said several years later that *How to Build Confidence in Your Child* was also *his* favourite of my writings. But to my great sorrow, we lost my dad on December 4, 1977. I miss him still and feel the void left by the deprival of his unique wisdom and guidance. How I would love to spend another afternoon walking with him in a cool park, sharing ideas or inspirations that have come since his departure. He was a wonderful man who played a significant part in shaping my values and attitudes – and in the preparation of this book. Perhaps it is now clear why I dedicated *How to Build Confidence in Your Child* to my father, James Dobson, Sr.

I hope you enjoy this book. But may I make one simple request while you are reading? Please don't yawn at me! I'm still not confident enough to take that response.

JAMES C. DOBOSN

Introduction

John McKay, the great football coach at the University of Southern California, was interviewed on television a few years ago, and the subject of his son's athletic talent was raised. John, Junior, was a successful player on his dad's team. Coach McKay was asked to comment on the pride he must feel over his son's accomplishments on the field. His answer was most impressive:

> Yes. I'm pleased that John had a good season last year. He does a fine job and I *am* proud of him. But I would be just as proud if he had never played the game at all.

Coach McKay was saying, in effect, that John's football talent is recognised and appreciated, but his human worth does not depend on his ability to play football. Thus, his son would not lose respect if the next season brought failure and disappointment. John's place in his dad's heart was secure, being independent of his performance. I wish every child could say the same.

To the contrary, human worth in our society is carefully reserved for those who meet certain rigid specifications. The beautiful people are born with it; those who are highly intelligent are likely to find approval; superstar athletes are usually respected. But no one is considered valuable just because he *is*! Social acceptability is awarded rather carefully, making certain to exclude those who are unqualified.

Believe it or not, a five-year-old is capable of 'feeling' his own lack of worth in this system. Most of our little ones have observed very early that some people are valuable and some aren't; they also know when they are one of the losers! In many ways, we parents inadvertently teach this system to them, beginning in infancy to place a price tag on human worth. The result is widespread inferiority and inadequacy – which has probably included you and me in its toll.

There is a better way! This book is intended to help parents and teachers raise self-confident, healthy children. Our youngsters need not *hide* in shame; by applying the strategies I have outlined, and others which parents can identify, we can give them the courage to *seek* the best from their world.

SCHOOL EDUCATION IN THE UNITED STATES

Age	Grade				
		Doctoral Degree 3-7 years		**Postgraduate Professional Schools: Law, Medicine, etc.**	**HIGHER EDUCATION**
	Senior Junior Sophomore	**Master's Degree** 1 or 2 years			
18	Freshman	**4-year Bachelor's Degree in College or University**			
		Junior College, 2-year Transfer or Vocational			
17	12th	**High School 4 Years**	**Senior High School 3 Years**		**SECONDARY EDUCATION**
16	11th				
15	10th				
14	9th		**Junior High School 3 Years**		
13	8th				
12	7th				
11	6th	**Elementary (Grade) School**			**PRIMARY EDUCATION**
10	5th				
9	4th				
8	3rd				
7	2nd				
6	1st				
5	Kindergarten	**Kindergarten**			
3/4		**Nursery Schools**			

HOW TO BUILD CONFIDENCE IN YOUR CHILD

1

THE EPIDEMIC OF INFERIORITY

He began his life with all the classic handicaps and disadvantages. His mother was a powerfully built, dominating
woman who found it difficult to love anyone. She had been
married three times, and her second husband divorced her
because she beat him up regularly. The father of the child
I'm describing was her third husband; he died of a heart
attack a few months before the child's birth. As a consequence, the mother had to work long hours from his
earliest childhood.

She gave him no affection, no love, no discipline, and no
training during those early years. She even forbade him to
call her at work. Other children had little to do with him, so
he was alone most of the time. He was absolutely rejected
from his earliest childhood. He was ugly and poor and un-
trained and unlovable. When he was thirteen years old a
school psychologist commented that he probably didn't even
know the meaning of the word 'love'. During adolescence,
the girls would have nothing to do with him and he fought
with the boys.

Despite a high IQ, he failed academically, and finally
dropped out during his third year of high school. He thought
he might find a new acceptance in the Marine Corps; they
reportedly built men, and he wanted to be one. But his
problems went with him. The other marines laughed at him
and ridiculed him. He fought back, resisted authority, and
was court-martialled and thrown out of the marines with an
undesirable discharge. So there he was – a young man in his

early twenties — absolutely friendless and shipwrecked. He was small and scrawny in stature. He had an adolescent squeak in his voice. He was balding. He had no talent, no skill, no sense of worthiness. He didn't even have a driving licence.

Once again he thought he could run from his problems, so he went to live in a foreign country. But he was rejected there too. Nothing had changed. While there, he married a girl who herself had been an illegitimate child and brought her back to America with him. Soon, she began to develop the same contempt for him that everyone else displayed. She bore him two children, but he never enjoyed the status and respect that a father should have. His marriage continued to crumble. His wife demanded more and more things that he could not provide. Instead of being his ally against the bitter world, as he hoped, she became his most vicious opponent. She could outfight him, and she learned to bully him. On one occasion, she locked him in the bathroom as punishment. Finally, she forced him to leave.

He tried to make it on his own, but he was terribly lonely. After days of solitude, he went home and literally begged her to take him back. He surrendered all pride. He crawled. He accepted humiliation. He came on her terms. Despite his meagre salary, he brought her seventy-eight dollars as a gift, asking her to take it and spend it any way she wished. But she laughed at him. She belittled his feeble attempts to supply the family's needs. She ridiculed his failure. She made fun of his sexual impotency in front of a friend who was there. At one point, he fell on his knees and wept bitterly, as the greater darkness of his private nightmare enveloped him.

Finally, in silence, he pleaded no more. No one wanted him. No one had ever wanted him. He was perhaps the most rejected man of our time. His ego lay shattered in a fragmented dust!

The next day, he was a strangely different man. He arose, went to the garage, and took down a rifle he had hidden there. He carried it with him to his newly acquired job at a book-storage building. And from a window on the sixth floor of that building, shortly after noon, November 22, 1963, he sent two shells crashing into the head of President John Fitzgerald Kennedy.

Lee Harvey Oswald, the rejected, unlovable failure, killed the man who, more than any other man on earth, embodied all the success, beauty, wealth, and family affection which he lacked. In firing that rifle, he utilised the *one* skill he had learned in his entire, miserable lifetime.

Oswald's personal problems do not excuse his violent behaviour, certainly, and I would not attempt to absolve him of the responsibility and blame. Yet an understanding of his inner torment and confusion helps us see him, not only as a vicious assassin, but also as the pitiful, broken man he became. Every day of his life, from the lonely days of childhood to the televised moment of his spectacular death, Oswald experienced the crushing awareness of his own inferiority. Finally, as it often does, his grief turned to anger.

The greater tragedy is that Lee Harvey Oswald's plight is not unusual in America today. While others may respond less aggressively, this same consuming awareness of inadequacy can be seen in every avenue of life – in every neighbourhood, in each church, and on the campuses of America's schools. It is particularly true of today's adolescents. I have observed that the vast majority of those between twelve and twenty years of age are bitterly disappointed with who they are and what they represent. In a world that worships superstars and miracle men, they look in the mirror for the signs of greatness, seeing only a terminal case of acne. Most of these discouraged young people will not admit how they feel because it hurts to acknowledge these inner thoughts. Oswald never published his early self-doubts and loneliness – nor would we have listened if he had. Thus, much of the rebellion, discontent, and hostility of the teenage years emanates from overwhelming, uncontrollable feelings of inferiority and inadequacy which rarely find verbal expression.

Teenagers are by no means alone in this personal devaluation. Every age poses its own unique threats to self-esteem. As I will discuss, little children typically suffer a severe loss of status during the tender years of childhood. Likewise, most adults are still attempting to cope with the inferiority experienced in earlier times. And I am convinced that senility and mental deterioration at the latter end of life often result from the growing awareness by the aged that they live in the exclusive world of the young; where wrinkles, backaches, and dentures are matters of scorn; where their ideas are out-of-date and their continued existence is a burden. This feeling of uselessness is the special reward that we reserve for life's survivors, and it should not be surprising that the elderly often 'disconnect' intellectually.

Thus, if inadequacy and inferiority are so universally prevalent at all ages of life at this time, we must ask ourselves 'why?' Why can't our children grow up accepting themselves as they are? Why do so many feel unloved and unlovable? Why are our homes and schools more likely to produce despair and self-hatred than quiet confidence and respect? Why should each child have to bump his head on the same old rock? These questions are of major significance to every parent who would shield his child from the agony of inferiority.

The current epidemic of self-doubt has resulted from a totally unjust and unnecessary system of evaluating human worth, now prevalent in our society. Not everyone is seen as worthy; not everyone is accepted. Instead, we reserve our praise and admiration for a select few who have been blessed from birth with the characteristics we value most highly. It is a vicious system, and we, as parents, must counterbalance its impact. This book is dedicated to the proposition that all children are created worthy and must be given the right to personal respect and dignity. It can be done!

In order to help parents understand what their children are facing, I have devoted the following two chapters to an analysis of the false values on which self-esteem so often depends in our culture. I hope the reader will see how effectively (and often unknowingly) we teach our small children that worthiness and social approval are beyond reach for them. Thus, by glorifying an idealised model to which few can conform, we have created a vast army of 'have-nots' – born losers who are discouraged with life before it has really begun. Like Lee Harvey Oswald, they turn this way and that, searching vainly for a solution to the inner emptiness and pain. For the millions who never find it, the road to personal worth becomes a long, unpaved detour leading nowhere.

The matter of personal worth is not only the concern of those who lack it. In a real sense, the health of an entire society depends on the ease with which its individual members can gain personal acceptance. *Thus, whenever the keys to self-esteem are seemingly out of reach for a large percentage of the people, as in twentieth-century America, then widespread 'mental illness', neuroticism, hatred, alcoholism, drug abuse, violence, and social disorder will certainly occur. Personal worth is not something human beings are free to take or leave. We must have it, and when it is unattainable, everybody suffers.*

But I have not written this book merely to discuss our problems – or even to criticise the society which creates them. Rather, I have proposed a better way. By a proper use of parental influence and direction, we can provide our children with the inner strength necessary to survive the obstacles they will face. We can open the road to self-esteem and personal worth. Perhaps we won't reconstruct the world, but we can certainly help our children cope with it more successfully.

The heart of this book, then, is devoted to a description of ten comprehensive 'strategies' for building self-esteem, each one focusing on a particular area of concern. These discussions offer specific answers and recommendations regarding the common threats to personal worth which surround our children. Some of the topics included are as follows:

Strategies for the early years
  • Building self-respect at home: the essence of good parenthood
  • Why 'love' is not enough

- The impact of fatigue and irritability
- Avoiding guilt in parenthood
- Shaping the will without breaking the spirit
- Preparing the child for the challenges ahead

Strategies for middle childhood
- Reducing educational threats to esteem
- Your child's *best* weapon against inferiority
- The impact of television
- Avoiding overprotection and dependency
- Helping your child compete in a competitive world

Strategies for adolescence
- Preparing for adolescence
- Understanding the adolescent experience
- Help for the rejected teenager
- Building healthy sexual attitudes
- Dealing with social pressure

Strategies for adulthood
- Self-esteem in adulthood
- Sources of depression in women
- Self-esteem and the Women's Lib movement
- 'Therapy' from giving to others

Following the discussion of these strategies, Chapter 5, is a useful and concise explanation of human behaviour. It describes the basic personality types of children and adults, making their inner motivation more understandable. This chapter is recommended to the parent who wants to comprehend the meaning behind the behaviour of his children, his spouse, his mother-in-law, his neighbour – or even himself. It is followed by Chapter 6, devoted to comments and observations.

Before we can resolve the problems which confront our children, however, we must understand the predicament they are facing. Let's move back, then, into the world of the young, examining the destructive value system which is taught so effectively throughout the formative years of life. Parents and teachers can contribute greatly to the self-respect of the next generation if they can genuinely empathise with little people – seeing what they see, hearing what they hear and feeling what they feel.

2

BEAUTY: THE GOLD COIN OF HUMAN WORTH

The television personality Johnny Carson once commented on the delicate situation which occurs when a new mother first shows you her ugly baby. What do you say, as she holds him up with pride? Carson concluded that the only safe remark is, 'My, that sure is a baby, isn't it?' He is absolutely right. Mom's ego is never so unprotected as in that moment, and the onlooker had better choose his words *very* carefully. Why? Because in our society, a beautiful baby is a much more valuable human being than an unattractive one.

Without question, the most highly valued personal attribute in our culture (and in most others) is physical attractiveness. Accordingly, the personal worth of a newborn infant is anxiously evaluated by his parents as they examine his body and its accessories. For this reason, it is not uncommon for a mother to be very depressed shortly after the birth of her first baby. She knew that most newborns are rather homely, but she hadn't expected such a disaster! In fact, she had secretly hoped to give birth to a grinning, winking, blinking, six-week-old Gerber baby, having four front teeth and rosy, pink cheeks. Instead, they hand her a red, toothless, bald, prune-faced, screaming little creature whom she often wants to send back. You see, the personal worth of that one-day-old infant is actually doubted by his parents. Soon afterward, however, Mom learns to appreciate that face that only a mother could love – but other people don't. And this point must be emphasised: *we adults respond very differently to an unusually beautiful child than to a particularly unattractive one, and that difference has a profound impact on a developing personality.* The pretty child is much more likely to see the world as warm and accepting; the ugly child is far better acquainted with the cold, steel eyes of rejection.

Beauty and the Baby

When my little girl was fifteen months of age, she had physical features which seemingly appealed to adults. Her mother dressed her attractively, and there was considerable warmth and affection shown to Danae wherever she went. People would hold her in their arms, tease her, and give her candy. The attention that she received is typically given to any child who is thought to be cute or attractive. It is neither sought nor earned; it is given spontaneously by the adult world. However, three months after her first birthday, she rearranged her features for the worse. I had driven home from the hospital at the end of a workday and was met by my wife in the driveway. She was holding our little girl in her arms, and they were both splattered with blood. My wife quickly told me the painful details: Danae was learning to run and her mother was playfully chasing her through the house; suddenly the little toddler darted to the left, losing her balance. She had fallen into the sharp edge of a table in the living room, catching her front tooth squarely as she went down. The tooth had been driven completely into her gums, appearing to be knocked out. The inside of her lip was slashed and cut and she looked terrible.

My daughter's permanent tooth was not due for six more years and could also have been damaged by the impact. Fortunately, however, the baby tooth refused to die. It gradually returned to its proper place and the wound healed with no long-term damage. In fact, that same incisor was to make three more unscheduled trips into the gums before giving up the ghost four years later; it demonstrated uncanny courage in hanging on despite the whacks and bumps it absorbed. By the time it finally turned loose, Danae considered her toothlessness to be a valuable status symbol in the neighbourhood. At the time of the accident, however, the situation appeared very discouraging.

Danae's head-on collision with the table had temporarily distorted the shape of her mouth, and since the cut was on the inner part of her lip, she appeared to have been born that way. All of the babyish appeal was now gone. The next evening, I took her with me to a store and had momentarily forgotten about her accident. But I noticed that people were responding differently to her than they had earlier. They would look at her, and then turn away. Instead of the warmth, love and tenderness previously offered to her, there was a rejection and coolness which they unconsciously demonstrated. They were not trying to be mean; they simply did not find her attractive any longer. I was irritated by their reaction because it revealed the injustice in our value system. How unfair, it seemed, to reward a child for something he had not earned, or worse, to destroy him for circumstances beyond his control. Yet a child who is attractively arranged usually profits from his good fortune from the moment of birth.

Beauty contests offering scholarships and prizes for gorgeous babies are now common, as if the attractive child didn't already have enough advantages awaiting him in life. This distorted system of evaluating human worth can be seen in a thousand examples. The reader may remember the tragic incident that occurred in Chicago several years ago, when eight student nurses were viciously murdered. The following day, a commentator was discussing the violent event on the radio, and he said, 'The thing that makes this tragedy much worse is that all eight of these girls were so attractive!' In other words, the girls were more valuable human beings because of their beauty, making their loss more tragic. If one accepts that statement, then the opposite is also true: the murders would have been less tragic if homely girls were involved. The conclusion, as written by George Orwell, is inescapable: 'All [people] are equal, but some [people] are more equal than others.'

Beauty and the Child

Very early in life, a child begins to learn the social importance of physical beauty. The values of his society cannot be kept from his little ears, and many adults do not even try to conceal their bias. It's a dull child who fails to notice that the ugly do not win Miss America contests; the ugly do not become cheerleaders; the ugly seldom star in movies; the ugly may not get married; the ugly have fewer friends; the ugly are less desirable!

It is surprising just how effectively we teach our small children to appreciate the beauty cult. In examining the traditional literature of childhood, I was amazed to see how many of the age-old stories centre around physical attractiveness in one form or another. Consider these examples:

(1) *The Ugly Duckling*. Here is a familiar story about an unhappy little bird who was rejected by the better-looking ducks. Symbolising the plight of every unattractive child, the ugly duckling was disturbed by his grotesque appearance. Fortunately for him, however, he had a beautiful swan inside which surfaced in young adulthood. (The story does not mention the ugly duckling who grew up to be an ugly duck!) How many children wait patiently for their beautiful swan to appear, seeing things go from bad to worse during adolescence?

(2) *Sleeping Beauty*. Why was this story not titled 'Sleeping Ugly'? Because the prince would not have awakened her with a gentle kiss! He would have let a homely little princess go on resting. Her beauty was an essential ingredient in the romantic tale.

(3) *Rudolph the Red-Nosed Reindeer*. Rudolph had a weird nose which caused him to be rejected by his fellow reindeer. They laughed and called him names. They wouldn't let poor Rudolph join in any reindeer games. This story has nothing to do with reindeer; it has *everything* to do with children. This is how they treat the physically peculiar. They are rejected and ridiculed. The only way the world's 'Rudolphs' can gain acceptance is to perform some miraculous feat, symbolised by the gallant sleigh ride in the snowstorm.

(4) *Dumbo the Elephant.* Dumbo was ridiculed for having big, floppy ears, until he used them to fly. The theme is remarkably similar to the plight of poor Rudolph. It appears repeatedly in the literature of the young because of its common occurrence in the lives of children, themselves.

(5) *Snow White and the Seven Dwarfs.* The evil queen asked the fateful question, 'Mirror, mirror on the wall, who's the fairest of them all?' I am still awed by the stupidity of her question considering all of the possibilities to which a magic mirror might respond! Yet the motivation behind her request is clear: the fairest of them all was the most noble, worthy person in the land. Perhaps she still reigns.

(6) *Cinderella.* The primary difference between Cinderella and her two wicked stepsisters was a matter of beauty. Any illustrated story of Cinderella will reveal that fact. Sure, Cinderella was ragged and uncombed, but the basic ingredient was there. It wasn't the pumpkin and the mice that shook up the prince when Cinderella arrived at the ball. You can bet she was a pretty little thing.

(7) This theme emphasising beauty not only appears in the fairy stories from long ago — current literature reflects it as well. The approved, fourth-grade reader, adopted as a California state textbook at one time carried a fairy story about three little girls. Two of the girls were very attractive, having beautiful hair and facial features. Because of their beauty, they were loved by the people and were given kingdoms in which to rule. The third little girl was very ugly. No one liked her because she was not pleasant to look at, and the people would not let her have a kingdom of her own. She was very unhappy and sad. The story ended on such a bright note, however, for this little girl was given a kingdom with the animals! Isn't that jolly? Her ugliness got her banished from the world of human beings, as it often does. Her physical deficiencies were described in considerable detail in the textbook, so that similar children in the classroom would be stared and pointed at. Why must we emphasise this unattainable attribute so vigorously at every level of our

society? The message is loud and clear: really worthy folks are beautiful people.

Most children are able to determine the relative worth of their own physical arrangement by the time they enter kindergarten. A thirty-six-year-old man told me recently, 'I was five years old when I realised I was ugly, and I've never been the same since.' His entire adult personality had been shaped (distorted) by that awful realisation.

Another man, then sixty years of age, described his reaction to the beauty cult in such graphic terms that I wrote down his exact comment. He said, 'I saw this clearly when I was twelve years old. I saw the injustice of it. I saw that it was nobody's fault, particularly, so I didn't get bitter about it. But I resigned myself to play the game of life with a short hand.'

If a child is odd or noticeably different, he has certainly heard about his 'deformity' from his friends and neighbours during pre-school days. Without meaning to hurt others, children can be terribly brutal to one another. Some youngsters feel it their personal mission in life to point out everyone else's flaws and deficiencies. The unusual or different boy or girl has been informed of his unique characteristics from his earliest recollection. Life can be very uncomfortable, indeed, for the child who is too fat or too thin, too tall or too short, or besieged by a tornado of freckles, or whose nose curves up or down or to one side, or whose skin is ruddy, or whose hair is too curly or too straight, or one who has big feet or a crossed eye, or protruding ears, or a large 'behind', or any other noticeable distortion. The child's emotional reaction operates according to the weakest link in the chain; that is, he can be physically perfect except for a single embarrassing feature, and he will worry about that one deficiency as though it were the only important thing in life.

As indicated above, the world of little people can be a vicious place, although this aspect of childhood is often forgotten by busy adults. Transport yourself for a moment, back into the world of the very young, where unconcealed aggression lies just below the surface at all times; where you may have to fight to defend your honour, even if it costs you your front teeth; where name-calling, ridicule, and rejection are hurled at the weak like poison darts; where self-esteem teeters on the brink of disintegration with each failure or mistake. This threatening aspect of childhood must be remembered if we hope to understand the next generation. Why, for example, would some children rather take forty lashes than go to a new school, or perform in front of their peers? They know, but cannot explain, the pain that other children can inflict on their unprotected egos.

The note reproduced below was given to me by the mother of a fourth-grade girl who found it on her desk. It was apparently written without provocation and illustrates the brutality with which one child can assault the self-esteem of another:

Awful Janet
Your the stinkest girl in this world. I hope you die but of course I suppose that's impossible. I've got some ideals.
1. Play in the road
2. Cut your throad
3. Drink poison
4. get drunk
5. knife yourself
Please do some of this you big fat Girl. we all hate you. I'm praying Oh please lord let Janet die. Were in need of fresh air. Did you hear me lord cause if you didn't will all die with her here. See Janet we're not all bad.
                                    From Wanda Jackson

What is 'Awful Janet' to think about a venomous note of this nature? She may have the self-confidence to take it in stride, particularly if Wanda is a social failure, herself. However, if Wanda is popular and Janet is not, the stage is set for a painful and enduring emotional experience. Notice that Wanda made reference to Janet's physical appearance ('you big fat Girl') and she implied that a vast army of friends agreed with her ('we all hate you'). Those two ingredients would crush a sensitive child.

It has always been surprising to me to witness the emotional power of such an episode. If Janet was stung by the note, it will probably be remembered all through her life. Ask any adult to relate a similar incident from childhood and you'll get an immediate response, describing an experience that may have occurred forty long years ago. When I was in the sixth grade, for example, a classmate called me 'skinny'. He said it only once, yet I remember the event perfectly today. I would still like to blacken his eye. Why? Because my personal worth was questioned! Likewise, a middle-aged man told me recently that he had been very self-conscious about his excessive height when he was in junior high school. His mother was asked how she could find him in a crowd, and she replied, 'I just look for the kid who's sticking up above everyone else.' Zap! The arrow stuck in his heart, and he remembers it three decades later. He has forgotten everything else that occurred that month, but he can still hear his mother's words ringing in his head. In a similar vein, the comedian George Carlin always hated his name because his friends would sing: 'Georgieporgie Puddininpie, Kissed the girls and made them cry; When the boys came out to play, Georgieporgie ran away.' George said he was painfully aware of the vague references to his manhood in this goading chant.

Youngsters are highly skilled at composing nicknames to replace the titles carefully selected by another child's parents. These names are seldom intentionally vicious, but their impact is often devastating. They are usually derived from the victim's primary physical flaw, spotlighting and emphasising the feature he'd most like to hide. Thus, the boy with protruding teeth becomes 'Bucky Beaver'; the plump fellow is 'Porker'; the hairy girl is 'Shag'; the skinny boy is 'Bones'; the skinny girl is 'Birdlegs'; the large-framed young lady is 'Moose'; the tiny boy is 'Runt' or 'Pee Wee' or 'Peanut', etc. Lee Harvey Oswald was called 'Ozzie Rabbit' in the Marine Corps; Joseph Stalin was called the 'nine-toed one', because of a fusion between two of his toes. The examples of this kind of disrespect are innumerable.

I knew a small boy in junior high school who had a round head, thick glasses (which caused his eyes to appear bulged), and a very large mouth. The other students called him 'Frog'. It was a perfect nickname, except that Frog himself wasn't so proud of the analogy. It never occurred to his classmates that he might not *want* to look like a little green creature on a lily pad. The ultimate insult came when they asked Frog if he could cause warts on their hands and catch flies with his tongue. My point is this: the child becomes his nickname. He sees himself in those terms and suffers accordingly. How can Frog or Bucky or Moose or Bones regard themselves with respect when their friends see them as deformed and ridiculous? If you asked them to write an honest appraisal of 'Who am I,' they would begin by describing that one feature which caused the greatest personal dissatisfaction.

Children are keenly aware of their relative worth among their classmates. There are numerous events which reveal their standing in this regard. Who, for example, is elected captain of the baseball team? Who is never even nominated? Who is chosen first in games and contests? Who is selected last? Who is invited to the important birthday parties? Who is excluded? How many Valentine cards does an unpopular child receive, compared to the superstars? There are many simple and direct ways to evaluate one's social worth, and some children draw the same conclusion from each assessment: 'I am a complete washout and a failure.'

Teachers and psychologists have a more sophisticated technique for sampling social status among children. It is called a sociogram. Each child in a classroom is asked to list the three children with whom he would most like to sit, and the three by whom he would not like to be placed. Without informing the class of the results, the teacher can then tally the choices and identify the 'stars' and the 'isolates'. A good teacher will then throw her support behind the rejected youngster. Unfortunately, however, teachers are products of the same society which moulds the values and attitudes of everyone else. They are often repelled by the physically unattractive child and drawn to the cutie. Certainly, every good teacher fights this inclination, some more successfully than others.

Two researchers, Ellen Berscheid and Elaine Walster, published their startling findings in an article, 'Beauty and the Best', in *Psychology Today* (March, 1972). Consider the impact of these biases against the homely youngster:

(1) Evidence seems to indicate that academic grades given to students are influenced by the attractiveness of the child.

(2) When shown a set of children's pictures and asked to identify the child who probably created the classroom disturbance (or some similar act of misconduct), adults were likely to select an unattractive child as the offender. Likewise, the ugly child was thought to be more dishonest than his cute peer. As the authors put it, 'For all the talk about character and inner values, we assume the best about pretty people. And from grade school on, there's almost no dispute about who's beautiful.'

(3) According to the findings of Karen Dion, the way an adult handles a discipline problem is related to the attractiveness of the child. In other words, the *same* misbehaviour is likely to be handled more permissively for the cute youngster and more severely for his ugly classmate.

(4) Most importantly (and correlating with my observations), the impact of physical attractiveness is well established in nursery school! Cute little three-year-olds already enjoy greater popularity among their peers. And unfortunately, certain physical features, such as fatness, are already recognised and disliked at this tender age.

What a distorted system of values we propagate! What irreparable damage is done to an ugly child whose parents do not intervene on his behalf. Every day he is confronted by his own awful inferiority and there is no escape. He can blame no one. He can change nothing. He can neither explain nor apologise. He can't even hide. Cruel voices follow him wherever he goes, whispering their evil messages in his childish ears: 'The other children don't like you; see, I told you you'd fail; you're different; you're foolish; they hate you; you're a failure; you're worthless!' As time passes, the voices get louder and louder, until their scream obliterates all other sounds in his adolescent mind: 'There's no hope; you are doomed!'

Beauty and the Adolescent

If physical attractiveness is considered important during childhood, it becomes supersignificant and all-consuming during adolescence. For a period of four to six years following puberty, the child's entire physical and emotional apparatus is focused on the exciting new world of sex. He thinks about it, dreams about it, fantasises about it, and too often sets out to do something about it. He is aflame with sexual curiosity, romanticism, and sheer biological passion. Now obviously, in this atmosphere of sexual tension, physical beauty outpaces all other values and ideals. The girl who is unusually attractive has the world at her feet. The handsome, athletic boy is king of the mountain. Most others, constituting the vast majority, look in the mirror with disgust and disdain.

Any adolescent who wants to measure his worth needs only to listen to the music which surrounds him. The lyrics will underscore the significance of beauty. A song of the sixties proclaimed, for example, 'If a girl isn't pretty like a Miss Atlantic City, she's Miss Nowhere U.S.A.' This is the brutal, one-point value system which characterises the competitive world of today's teenager. Another song asks the beautiful girl to walk a little slower when she walks by. The singer implying, I suppose, that the homely girl can hasten on past. A third song, somewhat older, poetically comments that a pretty girl is like a melody. If we accept this analogy, then who do you suppose is the sour note within the symphony of American values?

To help understand the predicament facing our kids, let's suppose that you are an adolescent girl at this moment. You are sixteen years old and your name is Helen Highschool. To be very honest, you are not exactly gorgeous. Your shoulders are rounded and you have trouble remembering to close your mouth when you're thinking. (That seems to worry your folks a lot.) There are pimples distributed at random over your forehead and chin, and your oversized ears keep peeking out from under the hair that should hide them. You think often about these flaws and have wondered, with proper reverence, why God wasn't paying attention when you were being assembled.

You have never had a real date in your life, except for that disaster last February. Your mom's friend, Mrs. Nosgood, arranged a blind date that almost signalled the end of the world. You knew it was risky to accept, but you were too excited to think rationally. Charming Charlie arrived in high spirits expecting to meet the girl of his dreams. You were not what he had in mind. Do you remember the disappointment on his face when you shuffled into the living room? Remember how he told Mary Lou the next day that your braces stuck out farther than your chest? Remember his saying you had so much bridgework in your mouth that he'd have to pay a toll to kiss you? Horrible! But the night of your date he didn't say anything. He just sulked through the evening and brought you home two hours early. Mary Lou couldn't wait to tell you the following afternoon how much Charlie hated you, of course. You lashed back in anger. You caught him in the hall and told him he wasn't too bright for a boy with a head shaped like a light bulb. But the hurt went deep. You despised all males for at least six months and thought your hormones would never make a comeback.

When you arrived home from school that afternoon, you went straight to your room without speaking to the family. You closed the door and sat on the bed. You thought about the injustice of it all, letting your young mind play hopscotch over many painful little memories that refused to fade. In fact, it seemed as though you were suddenly on trial to determine your acceptability to the human race.

The attorney for the prosecution stood before the jury and began presenting incriminating evidence as to your unworthiness. He recalled that fourth-grade Valentine's Day party when your beautiful cousin, Ann, got thirty-four cards and two boxes of candy, most of them from love-sick boys. You got three cards – two from girls and one from your Uncle Albert in San Antonio. The jury shook their heads in sorrow. The attorney then described the day that sixth-grade boy shared his ice-cream cone with Betty Brigden but said he'd 'catch the uglies' if you took a bite. You acted like you didn't hear him, but you went to the girls' rest room and cried until the recess was over.

'Ladies and Gentlemen of the jury,' said the attorney, 'these are the unbiased opinions of Helen's own generation. The entire student body of Washington High School obviously agrees. They have no reason to lie. Their views represent truth itself. This homely girl simply does not deserve to be one of us! I urge you to find her guilty this day!'

Then the attorney for the defence arose. He was a frail little man who stuttered when he spoke. He presented a few witnesses on your behalf, including your mom and dad – and Uncle Albert, of course.

'Objection, your honour!' shouted the prosecutor, 'These are members of her family. They don't count. They're biased witnesses, and their opinions are untrustworthy.' 'Objection sustained,' quoted the judge. Your attorney, flustered and disconcerted, then mentioned how you kept your room clean, and he made a big deal about that *A* you got on a geography test last month. You saw the foreman of the jury suppress a yawn and the others showed signs of complete boredom.

'A-a-and so, l-l-ladies and gentlemen of the j-j-jury, I ask y-y-you to find this y-y-young lady in-innocent of the charges.'

The jury was gone for thirty-seven seconds before bringing in a verdict. You stood before them and recognised them all. There was last year's Homecoming Queen. There was the quarterback of the football team. There was the valedictorian of the senior class. There was the surgeon's handsome son. They all looked down at you with stern eyes, and suddenly shouted in one voice: 'GUILTY AS CHARGED, YOUR HONOUR!' The judge then read your sentence:

Helen Highschool, a jury of your peers has found you to be unacceptable to the human race. You are hereby sentenced to a life of loneliness. You will probably fail in everything you do, and you'll go to your grave without a friend in the world. Marriage is out of the question, and there will never be a child in your home. You are a failure, Helen. You're a disappointment to your parents and must be considered excess baggage from this point forward. This case is hereby closed.

The dream faded, but the decision of the jury remained real. Your parents wondered why you were so irritable and mean during the weeks that followed. They never knew – and you didn't tell them – that you had been expelled from the world of the Beautiful People.

I wish I could talk to all the Helens and Bobs and Suzies and Jacks who have also been found unacceptable in the courtroom of the mind. They may never know that the trial was rigged – that every member of the jury has been charged with the same offence – that the judge himself was convicted more than thirty years ago. I wish I could tell each discouraged teenager that we have all stood before that bar of injustice, and few have been acquitted. Some of the adolescent convicts will be 'pardoned' later in life, but a greater number will never escape the sentence of the judge! And the irony of it all is that we *each* conduct our *own* rigged trial. We serve as our own prosecutor, and the final sentence is imposed under our own inflexible supervision – with a little help from our 'friends', of course.

Beauty and the Adult

I am sitting at this moment near the guest swimming pool,

Sheraton Hotel, Waikiki Beach, Hawaii. (If one must write, he may as well enjoy the process.) The beautiful pool is virtually deserted, although around its borders lie several hundred narcissistic body-worshippers. They are a curious lot, when one stops to examine them. Each one clutches a bottle of suntan lotion, and rotates his flesh systematically under the burning sun. They remind me of giant rotisseries, baking themselves evenly on all sides. They endure this monotonous activity for hours, checking their colour regularly and comparing it with others near by. Medical science has told them that this solar exposure will wrinkle them like prunes within a few years, but no matter. They are in hot pursuit of instant beauty and it is worth the cost. (Incidentally, the Women's Lib spokesmen say females are tired of being treated like sex objects, but I can see no evidence of that weariness here.)

But all is not well among the older set. In addition to the physical worries of children and teenagers, we adults have another formidable enemy to combat: ageing! It is said that time is not a thief; it is an embezzler, juggling the books at night so we won't notice anything is missing. Then suddenly, at about thirty years of age, Mr. Young begins to realise that everything is gradually turning loose. He presses his face close to the mirror and examines the new signs of deterioration. He's been hit by the well-known triple threat: sag, wrinkle, and droop! The pull of gravity is steadily destroying his jawline, and there is no way to anchor it in place. Most of the musculature which once rippled across his chest has now melted and skidded down toward his protuding stomach. A little more of his precious hair defects to the pillow each night, eventually leaving nothing above his ears but skin and bone. His wife can hardly console him – she has troubles of her own. She brags to her husband that she still has the body of a twenty-year-old, and he replies, 'Well, give it back, you're getting it all wrinkled.' (The middle-aged woman who still has her 'schoolgirl figure' was probably a pretty dumpy kid.) It was just a joke, but it struck home. In her panic to preserve what is left, she rushes to the pharmacist and buys bee jelly and horse hormones – anything, in fact, which promises to tighten, mask, and undergird that which is sliding. But alas, her careful reconstruction washes off each evening, leaving the same old grooves and lines and bags and bumps. She then bakes it in the sun and jiggles it in the gym, but nothing helps for long. Obviously, this inevitable process of ageing is extremely painful to a beauty worshipper, whether masculine or feminine.

Having tried everything else, American women are rushing to their plastic surgeons in record numbers, enduring considerable pain and expense to roll back the years. And surprisingly, research shows that at least half of the working women who get a face-lift can expect to receive salary increases in the months that follow. It is clear that beauty is a highly marketable commodity in the business world. Most bosses seek attractive secretaries and receptionists, whereas homely women often find it difficult to obtain a job of any kind.

Most of the major choices made by adults are influenced one way or another by the attribute of beauty. A half-inch of flesh on the end of a woman's nose, for example, would likely rearrange her entire life, particularly affecting her selection of (or by) a marital partner. Each of us possesses a certain amount of physical bargaining power for use in romantic ventures, and most men attempt to 'capture' a mate with the greatest possible beauty. A very attractive spouse is a highly desirable prize to be displayed. As they say, 'If at first you don't succeed, try someone a little homelier.'

Unattractive men do not escape the discrimination I've described. Ugly salesmen are less successful than their handsome competitors. Homely politicians are asked to kiss fewer babies – and we all know what that means on election day. But perhaps the most common form of masculine discrimination is directed against the short man, who faces lifelong disadvantages. It is interesting to note that the taller of two American presidential candidates has won every election since 1900, with the exception of Calvin Coolidge in 1924 and Richard Nixon in 1972. (Someone commented that both those choices were mistakes, but I'll leave that matter to the reader.)

Adults are hardly immune to the tyranny of the beauty cult, even though they're old enough to know better. There is life after twenty-nine, and it's time we recognised it.

Beauty and the Elderly

Those of us who are younger cannot possibly appreciate the full implications of being part of the Unwanted Generation; to be aged in a time dominated by the very young; to be unable to see or hear well enough; to have an active mind hopelessly trapped in an inactive body; to be dependent on busy children; to be virtually sexless, emotionally and physically, in an eroticised society; to be unable to produce or contribute anything really worthwhile; to have no one who even remembers your younger days. This is inferiority at its worst! And as I stated in the first chapter, I am certain that many of the physical illnesses of old age are triggered by such feelings of worthlessness. A gastroenterologist (medical specialist in stomach and intestinal problems) told me recently that eighty percent of his older patients have physical symptoms caused by emotional problems. They feel unneeded and unloved, and their despair is quickly translated into bodily disorders. Obviously, love and esteem are essential to human life at all ages.

Conclusion

I have not written the preceding description to create parental discouragement and despondency. There is much room for hope and optimism for the family which acts to counterbalance these harmful forces on behalf of their children. However, for the past twenty years, the tendency among American parents has been to 'farm out' more and more elements of parental responsibility. We ask the child-care centre, the nursery school, the elementary educators, and the church to assume many of the instructional tasks which were previously handled by the family. A popular theme in recent literature has been, 'How to be a good parent in your spare time,' appealing to this notion that effective childrearing is duck soup for the parent who organises and delegates properly. But the building of self-esteem in your child is one responsibility which cannot be delegated to others. The task is too difficult and too personal to be handled in group situations. Without your commitment and support, Junior is on his own against formidable foes. With few exceptions, our materialistic society is not going to reinforce healthy self-concepts in your children, and if these desirable attitudes are to be constructed – only you can do it. No one else will care enough to make the necessary investment. This book is devoted to helping parents and teachers achieve that objective.

Questions and Answers

(1) *Why do people seem to be more conscious of their physical flaws and inadequacies now than in the past? What accounts for the 'epidemic' of inferiority which you described?*

I believe this tremendous emphasis on physical attractiveness is a by-product of the sexual revolution going on around us. Our society has been erotically supercharged since the midsixties when the traditional moral standards and restraints began to collapse. Television, radio, magazines, movies, billboards, literature, and clothing all reflect this unparalleled fascination with sensuality of various sorts. Now obviously, when sex becomes all-important in a society, as we are witnessing, then each person's sex appeal and charm take on new social significance. Simply stated, the more steamed up a culture becomes over sex, the more it will reward beauty and punish ugliness.

The need to be sexually attractive has become so powerful in America today that each person is expected to maximise his own seductiveness. When in our history have so many women had their hair professionally maintained each week?

When have so many men bought and used expensive cosmetics? When have so many parents struggled to find the right hairstyle for their children? These factors reflect social pressure of the highest magnitude. Women, particularly, are urged by a billion-dollar beauty industry to conceal their physical flaws and reveal most everything else, regardless of the cost involved.

I have always enjoyed 'people watching' on a busy sidewalk, noting how diligently each passerby has worked on his exterior that day. Some of the reconstructed faces must take hours to assemble before the mirror each morning, particularly when Mother Nature did a sloppy job in the beginning. I know a vain physician, for example, whose patients do not suspect that he is almost totally bald. He retains a patch of hair around the ears and neck, which has now grown to ten or more inches in length. Each morning the self-concious doctor weaves it all together on the top of his head and glues it down with hair spray. He obviously knows that bald-headed doctors are 'seen' differently than hairy ones – and hairy is better!

During a visit to Europe in 1972, I looked closely for evidence of the same body awareness among the natives, but it was not as apparent. The women were no less attractive than American women, but they had obviously not invested the same effort in perfecting their physical endowment. (I also observed that there must be a great shortage of razor blades in those hirsute countries.)

Any advertiser worth his salt knows that sex and beauty are the sensitive nerves on which to romp, and he must somehow link his products to those motivations, regardless of how contrived the connection might be. We're sold toothpaste that grants sex appeal (how foolish!), and breakfast cereal that makes us better looking (let's all have a bowl), and mints that guarantee a second kiss, and a bath-oil product for ladies which proclaims, 'If he doesn't feel the difference, he has no fuse.' (Her husband doesn't know it, but his entire manhood will be on the line the next time he touches her rejuvenated skin.) She is promised that she isn't getting 'older', she's getting 'better' — (and isn't that ridiculous?) There is no way to estimate the number of dollars spent each year to make us more competitive in an eroticised society.

In summary, it is my view that the increased sensuality in America during the seventies is generating a higher incidence of emotional casualties among people who are intensely aware of their inability to compete in the flirtatious game. If beauty represents the necessary currency (the gold coin of worth), then they are undeniably bankrupt. And sadly, the most vulnerable victims of this foolish measure of human worth are the little children who are too young to understand, too immature to compensate, and too crushed to fight back.

(2) *What are the prospects for the very pretty or handsome child? Does he usually have smooth sailing all the way?*

He has some remarkable advantages, as I have described. He is much more likely to accept himself and enjoy the benefits of self-confidence. However, he also faces some unique problems which the homely child never experiences. Beauty in our society is power, and power can be dangerous in immature hands. A fourteen-year-old nymphette, for example, who is prematurely curved and rounded in all the right places may be pursued vigorously by males who would exploit her beauty. As she becomes more conscious of her flirtatious power, she is sometimes urged towards early promiscuity. Furthermore, women who have been coveted physically since early childhood, such as Marilyn Monroe or Brigitte Bardot, may become bitter and disillusioned by the depersonalisation of body worship.

Research also indicates some interesting consequences in regard to marital stability for the 'beautiful people'. In one important study, the more attractive college girls were found to be less happily married twenty-five years later. It is apparently difficult to reserve the 'power' of sex for one mate, ignoring the ego gratification which awaits outside the marriage bonds. And finally, the more attractive a person is in his youth, the more painful is the ageing process.

My point is this: the measurement of worth on a scale of beauty is wrong, often damaging both the 'haves' and the 'have-nots'.

3

INTELLIGENCE: THE SILVER COIN OF HUMAN WORTH

When the birth of a first-born child is imminent, his parents pray that he will be normal — that is, 'average'. But from that moment on, average will not be good enough.

The Parental View

If beauty represents the primary ingredient of self-esteem and worthiness, the second most important attribute in our culture is certainly intelligence. Shortly after examining their baby's eyes, ears, nose, and related appendages for imperfections, most new parents begin looking for the signs of budding genius. And believe it or not, they seem to find it! A child's growth and development are so rapid during the first year of life that his awestruck parents watch their 'brilliant' creation in amazement. 'Only eight months ago the kid was completely helpless; now look at him! He said "Mama" six full weeks before the average child; this kid's got a real head on his shoulders.' They give him credit for having smiled at five days of age, when in reality 'the kid' was grimacing from severe wind.

As their child steamrolls into his second year of life, evidence mounts that he is intellectually loaded. What his parents may not know is that human mental awakening is thrilling, even for the average youngster. Every day, it seems, something new is learned or mimicked. This normal process is terribly exciting to those who are watching for the first time. How many parents have said to me with blatant pride:

'You wouldn't believe how that boy can think and reason; he remembers things I told him weeks ago.' They would estimate his IQ to be somewhere between 180 and 240, depending on his willingness to cooperate. They start saving their money for his college education.

Then come the 'terrible twos' and Junior learns the meaning of one word much better than all others – 'No!' He is impossible to handle and wants his own way in everything he does. His parents find him a pain and a trial, but they are secretly proud that he is going to be an independent thinker and a leader. 'Look how he pushes the other children around! This kid isn't going to be a follower, you can sure see that.'

Time will prove, however, that Junior's parents have drawn some premature and unwarranted conclusions. As he reaches his third, fourth, and fifth birthdays, he appears less and less remarkable. Mom and Dad begin to have some nagging doubts about the new genius in their family. In fact, much of his behaviour seems depressingly ordinary. He is often giddy, noisy and characteristically childish in his manner. He would much rather play than work and he has still not learned to read. At last he skips off to kindergarten, and the golden image called 'superchild' suddenly turns suspiciously green.

The first 'open house' night is a devastating experience for Junior's loving parents. They are tense as cats when they arrive at school, facing the unknown verdict. For six weeks their pudgy little pride and joy has been out there beyond their reach. *What* has he been doing? Whether they will admit it or not, their reputation as 'good parents' is on the line. If Junior has been a brat, then their discipline is faulty. If he has refused to work, they are guilty of teaching him irresponsibility. But worse, if he appears dumb, they must have endowed him with inferior mental equipment. Their egos are inextricably wrapped around this firstborn child; his mistakes, failures, and blunders send barbed arrows into their backsides. They glance quickly around the classroom to the place where children's work is exhibited, but Junior's paper isn't there. Then they see it, down in the lower corner of the bulletin board, very near the floor. It is awful! They blush at the unbelievably sloppy mess. That couldn't be his! But it has his misspelled name on it. Just then, Miss Dingle comes over to meet Junior's parents. She is pleasant and professional, smiling and winking and explaining her programme. They nervously ask her how Junior is doing, and she hangs a two-second pause that is pregnant with meaning. 'Well,' Miss Dingle begins, 'I've been intending to get in touch with you. . . .'

Not all parents overestimate the intellectual potential of their children, as did Junior's parents. Some experience tremendous anxiety over their child's early slowness and immaturity. They have memorised the average ages at which children typically learn to sit up, crawl, eat with a spoon, say Da Da, and throw string beans, and they know that their little butterball is behind in too many areas. The unspeakable fear of mental retardation hovers over them day-by-day, and they await each developmental milestone with unconcealed tension.

Whether parents overestimate or underestimate the mental potential of their children, it is obvious that most of them are highly sensitive and vulnerable regarding the matter of intelligence. Therefore, it is appropriate that we ask, why is there so much tension associated with the brain power of the next generation? Simply this: *intelligence is another extremely critical attribute in evaluating the worth of a child, second only to beauty in its importance*. These two qualities are not merely desirable features that we *hope* our children will possess. They rank at the very top of our value system above every imaginable alternative. When either characteristic is missing in a child, his parents often experience the agony, guilt, and disappointment of having produced an inferior child, a creation with the same intolerable flaws which they have long despised in themselves.

I talked recently with a family that applied for the adoption of a child. They had finally received the long-awaited telephone call, informing them that a baby had been selected for their consideration. The father told me how he questioned the representative from the adoption agency about the infant's history and heritage:

'Did his mother use drugs during pregnancy?'

'How intelligent are the parents?'

'How tall were they?'

'How well did they do in school?'

'What do they look like?'

'Is any hereditary disease evident in them?'

'What was the nature of the pregnancy and delivery?'

'How long did labour last?'

'What did the obstetrician say in his report?'

'Has the child been seen by a pediatrician?'

During the course of this intense questioning, however, the father began to feel guilty about his motives.

'I realised,' he said, 'that I was inspecting and evaluating this child as if I were buying a new automobile. I was actually asking if this baby boy was "qualified" to become my son. I suddenly comprehended that the infant lying there before me was a magnificent human being, regardless of any flaws and disadvantages. He was the creation of God Himself, who had given him an immortal soul, yet there I stood demanding a perfect child who could become a personal credit to me.'

This father's attitude toward his adopted son is observed frequently in the reaction of natural parents, as well. When the birth of their firstborn child draws near, they hope and pray that the baby will be normal – that is, 'average'. But from that moment on, average will not be good enough. Their child must excel. He must succeed. He must triumph. He must be the first of his age to walk or talk or ride a tricycle. He must earn a stunning report card and amaze his teachers with his wit and wisdom. He must star in Little League, and later on he must be the quarterback or the senior class president or the valedictorian. His sister must be the cheerleader or the soloist or the homecoming queen. Throughout the formative years of childhood, his parents give him the same message day after day: 'We're counting on you to do something fantastic, Son, now don't disappoint us!'

According to Martha Weinman Lear, author of *The Child Worshippers*, the younger generation is our most reliable status symbol. Middle-class parents vigorously compete with each other in raising the best-dressed, best-fed, best-educated, best-mannered, best-medicated, best-cultured, and best-adjusted child on the block. The hopes, dreams, and ambitions of an entire family sometimes rest on the shoulders of an immature child. And in this atmosphere of fierce competition, the parent who produces an intellectually gifted child is clearly holding the winning sweepstakes ticket. As Lear says, 'By the present line of thinking all children deserve the very best except the [intellectually] gifted, who deserve even better.'

Unfortunately, exceptional children are just that — exceptions. Seldom does a five-year-old memorise the King James Version of the Bible, or play chess blindfolded, or compose symphonies in the Mozart manner. To the contrary, the vast majority of our children are not dazzlingly brilliant, extremely witty, highly coordinated, tremendously talented, or universally popular! They are just plain kids with oversized needs to be loved and accepted as they are. Thus, the stage is set for unrealistic pressure on the younger generation and considerable disappointment for their parents.

The Child's View

As stated in the last chapter, children already understand the importance of physical attractiveness by the time they are three or four years of age. Every conceivable educational resource is mobilised to drill home the necessity of 'looking good'. Fortunately, however, the second essential human attribute, intelligence, is much more subtle in its impact. The child with low-average ability does not have his IQ tattooed on his forehead, and he often survives the preschool years with his self-respect intact. In fact, he may be five or six years old before he notices the vast differences between himself and his brighter friends. Then it happens! He begins his school career and the whole world cracks and splinters in slow motion.

Make no mistake about it! School is a dangerous place for children with fragile egos. For the slow child, the typical setting is unintentionally programmed to disassemble his self-esteem, bit by bit, until nothing remains but broken pieces. Having been a teacher, I am well acquainted with the many ways self-esteem is innocently assaulted in the classroom. For example, Miss Lodestar announces to her students that they are going to have an arithmetic contest. The ever-popular Johnny and Mary are asked to serve as captains, choosing team members alternately. Mary is granted first-draft choice and she grabs the ranking intellectual superstar, who moves to the side of the room nearest the captain. Johnny's first choice also goes to a kid with exceptional brain power. Through this entire process, dumb little Arnie is slumped down in his seat, knowing trouble is coming. He's thinking, 'Somebody take me!' But Arnie can't even read – much less do maths – and everyone knows he's stupid. The captains go on choosing until there's nobody left in the centre of the room except Arnie, the local dummy. Johnny says. 'You take him,' and Mary says, 'No! You take him.' Finally Miss Lodestar orders Johnny to include Arnie on his team. And sure enough, when the contest begins, guess who flubs up? Guess who causes his team to lose? Guess who wishes he could curl up and die?

Arnie's learning problem is one of five common academic difficulties, each leading its victim to believe he is stupid – and of course, unworthy. They are illustrated as follows:

(1) *The Slow Learner*. Arnie, the child described above, is a slow learner – a very slow learner. No one knows why, least of all Arnie. He tries to do the work but nothing turns out right. He can't read. He doesn't understand science. He rarely receives a 'happy face' for doing things properly, and *never* has his teacher written 'Nice work, Arnie' on his paper. He is the only child in the room who won't get a gold star on his spelling chart.

Does all this bad news escape Arnie's observation? Certainly not! He isn't that slow. How foolish he feels! There is no explanation he can offer. He is utterly defenceless. He must sit there in front of everybody and fail, day after day. Consequently, something precious is dying inside Arnie. Oh, he'll go on living, but the youthful enthusiasm and excitement will soon be extinguished. Several decades from now, people will wonder why Arnie is such a bore – such an uncreative, insecure bore. And no one will be there to tell them that his light went out when he was six years of age.

(2) *The Semilliterate Child.* Martha is a seven-year-old Mexican-American girl who is repeating the first grade. She is semilliterate (often erroneously called bilingual). Two languages are spoken in her home, but she has learned neither of them very well. She is so incapable of expressing herself that she feels incredibly stupid. That is why she never makes a sound unless utterly compelled to talk. Silence is her only defence against the hostile world around her.

(3) *The Underachiever.* Sherrie is a bright young lady. Her IQ places her within the upper ten per cent of her classmates, and she can handle most academic tasks with ease. Unfortunately, Sherrie is very unself-disciplined by nature. She is easily distracted, frequently bored, and seldom motivated. She does her work as quickly as possible just to get it finished, and avoids any unnecessary effort. Homework is out of the question, and she effectively conceals from her parents what is required there. Every attempt to get Sherrie moving is followed by yet another burst of inertia. Furthermore, she doesn't *know* she is bright. The comments on her work papers give no clue as to her ability, since they merely reflect her sloppiness and inaccuracy. Her parents and teacher are obviously displeased with her performance, and Sherrie is likely to draw the same conclusion as her less able friends: 'I am dumb!'

(4) *The Culturally Deprived Child.* Willie is a black child from an impoverished neighbourhood. He has never visited a zoo, or ridden on a plane, or been fishing. His daddy's identity is a mystery and his mother works long hours to support five little children. His vocabulary is miniscule,

except for an astounding array of slang words, and he has no place to read or study at home. Willie *knows* he isn't going to make it in school, and this fact is already influencing his personal evaluation.

(5) *The Late Bloomer*. Finally, I want you to meet Donald, who is a 'late bloomer'. To understand his story, we must return to his preschool days.

Donald is five years old and will soon go to kindergarten. He is an immature little fellow who is still his mamma's baby in many ways. Compared to his friends, Donald's language is childish and his physical coordination is gross. He cries three or four times a day, and other children take advantage of his innocence. A developmental psychologist or a pediatrician would verify that Donald is neither physically ill nor mentally retarded; he is merely progressing on a slower physiological time-table than most children his age. Nevertheless, Donald's fifth birthday has arrived, and everyone knows that middle-class five-year-olds go to kindergarten. He is looking forward to school, but deep inside he is rather tense about this new challenge. He knows his mother is anxious for him to do well in school, although he doesn't really know why. His father has told him he will be a 'failure' if he doesn't get a good education. He's not certain what a failure is, but he sure doesn't want to be one. Mom and Dad are expecting something outstanding from him and he hopes he won't disappoint them. His sister Pamela is in the second grade now; she is doing well. She can read and print her letters and she knows the names of every day in the week. Donald hopes he will learn those things too.

Kindergarten proves to be tranquil for Donald. He rides the tricycle and pulls the wagon and plays with the toy clock. He prefers to play alone for long periods of time, provided his teacher, Miss Moss, is near by. It is clear to Miss Moss that Donald is immature and unready for the first grade, and she talks to his parents about the possibility of delaying him for a year. 'Flunk kindergarten?!' says his father. 'How can the kid flunk kindergarten?' Miss Moss tried to explain that Donald has not failed kindergarten: he merely needs another year to develop before entering the first grade. The suggestion sends his father into a glandular upheaval. 'The kid is six years old; he should be learning to read and write. What good is it doing him to drag around that dumb wagon and ride on a stupid tricycle? Get the kid in the first grade!' Miss Moss and her principal reluctantly comply.

The following September Donald clutches his Mickey Mouse lunch pail and walks on wobbly legs to the first grade. From day one he begins to have academic trouble, and reading seems to be his biggest source of difficulty. His new teacher, Miss Fudge, introduces the alphabet to her class, and Donald realises that most of his friends have already learned it. He has a little catching up to do. But too quickly Miss Fudge begins teaching something new; she wants the class to learn the sounds each letter represents, and soon he is even further behind. Before long, the class begins to read about Dick and Jane and their immortal dog 'Spot'. Some children can zing right along, but Donald is still working on the alphabet. Miss Fudge divides the class into three reading groups according to their initial skill. She wants to conceal the fact that one group is doing more poorly than the others, so she gives them the camouflage names of 'Lions', 'Tigers', and 'Giraffes'. Miss Fudge's motive is noble, but she fools no one. It takes the students about two minutes to realise that the Giraffes are all stupid! Donald begins to worry about his lack of progress, and the gnawing thought looms that there may be something drastically wrong with him.

During the first parent-teacher conference in October, Miss Fudge tells Donald's parents about his problems in school. She describes his immaturity and his inability to concentrate or sit still in the classroom.

'Nonsense,' says his father. 'What the kid needs is a little drill.' He insists that Donald bring him his books, allowing father and son to sit down for an extended academic exercise. But everything Donald does irritates his father. His childish mind wanders and he forgets the things he was told five minutes before. As his father's tension mounts, Donald's productivity descends. At one point, Donald's father crashes his hand down on the table and calls his son 'Stupid!' The child will never forget that knifing assessment.

Whereas Donald struggled vainly to learn during his early days in school, by November he has become disinterested and unmotivated. He looks out of the window. He draws and doodles with his pencil. He whispers and plays. Since he can't read, he can neither spell, nor write, nor do his social studies. He is un-involved and bored, not knowing what is going on most of the time. He feels fantastically inferior and in-adequate. 'Please stand, Donald, and read the next paragraph,' says his teacher. He stands and shifts his weight from foot to foot as he struggles to identify the first word. The girls snicker and he hears one of the boys say, 'What a dummy!' The problem began as a develop-mental lag, but has now become an emotional time bomb and a growing hatred for school.

Donald's story is from *Dare to Discipline* by Dr. James Dobson. Copyright © 1970, Tyndale House Publishers, Wheaton, Illinois. Used by permission.

The categories of learning problems which I've described (slow learner, semilliterate, underachiever, culturally de-prived, and late bloomer) represent the five large groups of students who consistently fail in the classroom. *It is appalling to recognise that the children in these five categories actually outnumber those students who feel successful in school!* This means that personal dissatisfaction and disappointment are very com-mon products of our educational system. It accounts for the large percentage of adults in our society who secretly 'know' they are stupid – the one lesson learned best from their school days.

As stated earlier, if we are to understand our children – their feelings and behaviour – then we must sharpen our memories of our own childhood. Can you, the reader, recall the agonising moments when you felt incredibly dumb as a child? Can you feel, even today, the rush of hot blood to your ears and neck when you blundered into a social mistake? Do you remember withering under a deafening guffaw after you had said something foolish at school? Is it possible to feel, one more time, the sting of ridicule and disrespect from the whole world? Every child experiences uncomfortable moments like these, but alas, some youngsters live with disgrace every day of their lives. The child with less than average ability is often predestined for this maelstrom of despair.

Other Components of Self-Esteem

I have emphasised the critical importance of two factors, beauty and intelligence, in shaping self-esteem and confidence. For men, physical attractiveness gradually submerges as a value during late adolescence and early adulthood, yielding first place to intelligence. For women, however, beauty retains its number one position throughout life, even into middle age and beyond. *The reason the average woman would rather have beauty than brains is because she knows the average man can see better than he can think*. Her value system is based on his and will probably continue that way. A man's personal preferences are also rooted in the opinions of the opposite sex, since most women value intelligence over handsomeness in men.

Certainly, beauty and intelligence are not the only ingredients in self-esteem. We have all known attractive intellectuals who could not conceal their own personal dissatisfaction. My point has been, simply, that inferiority is most often related to these two important values. A few of the other common influences are as follows:

(1) Parents have a remarkable power to preserve or damage the self-esteem of a child. Their manner either conveys respect and love or disappointment and disinterest. This parental role is discussed in greater detail in the strategies which follow.

(2) Older siblings can crush the confidence of a younger, weaker child. The little one can never run as fast, or fight as well, or achieve as much as his big brothers and sisters. And if his words are perpetually matters of scorn, he can easily conclude that he is foolish and incapable.

(3) Early social blunders and mistakes are sometimes extremely painful, being remembered throughout a lifetime.

(4) Financial hardship, depriving a child of the clothes and lifestyle of his peers, can cause a child to feel inferior. It is not the poverty, itself, which does the damage. Rather, it is the relative comparison with others. It is possible to feel deprived when you are truly rich by the world's standards. Incidentally, money is probably the third most important source of self-esteem in our culture. In the materialistic eyes of society, for example, a pimply-faced teenager on a bicycle is somehow less worthy than a pimply-faced teenager in a Datsun 240Z.

(5) Disease, even when unapparent, may represent the child's 'inner flaw'. A cardiac condition, or other disorder, which forces Mom to nag and beg him to go slow can convince a child that he is brittle and defective.

(6) A child who has been raised in a protected environment, such as a farm or a foreign missionary outpost, may be embarrassed by his undeveloped social skills. His tendency is to pull inward in shy withdrawal.

(7) Embarrassing family characteristics, such as having an alcoholic father or a mentally retarded sibling, can produce feelings of inferiority through close identification with the disrespected relatives.

Unfortunately, this list could be almost endless. In working with the problem of inadequacy, I have drawn this conclusion: whereas a child can lose self-esteem in a thousand ways, the careful reconstruction of his personal worth is usually a slow, difficult process.

Questions and Answers

(1) *Isn't there some indication that young people are also fed up with the values you have described?*

Yes, for a relatively short period of time during late adolescence. In fact, I believe the 'youth movement' during the last fifteen years, beginning with the beatniks, followed by the flower children and the hippies, and now composing the current counterculture, has been motivated by a rejection of the unreachable values I've described.

Sir Isaac Newton's third law of physics states: 'For every action there is an equal and opposite reaction.' His time-honoured observation not only describes matter in the physical realm, but applies to the world of people, too. Whenever a society emphasises one set of values far above its actual importance, there will soon be an appropriate 'equal and opposite' reaction among the dissenters: The youth movement, it seems clear, is that opposing response to the unparalleled stress on beauty, intelligence, and money. Consider the behaviour of the social dropout, referred to generally as a 'hippie'. He attempts to be as ugly as possible, often characterised by unkempt hair and the absence of makeup worn by females. He rejects formal education of all varieties, refusing to apply his intellectual potential in the traditional manner. ('You can lead your son to college but you can't make him think.') And finally, he spurns the entire work ethic whereby materialism is generated. It is my opinion that this protest behaviour is primarily motivated by a distaste for the values of the Establishment.

(2) *Is this a healthy trend?*

The rejection of our false values is an admirable viewpoint, in itself, but the larger question involves the substitutes which have taken their place. In the search for alternative values, many disillusioned young people have embraced drug abuse, venereal disease, filth, immorality, and a do-your-own-thing philosophy – which can hardly be considered improvements on the old system.

(3) *Does this account for the absence of meaning and purpose among so many young people?*

In a large measure, yes. I think it also explains the tremendous energy invested in the Jesus Movement during the late sixties. The principles of Christianity were suddenly rediscovered by the young at a time when all other values had faded and splintered. Into the vacuum came something truly worth living for – or even dying for. Here was a system of values that offered ultimate human worth and dignity to every person on earth. In retrospect, it seems inevitable that Christianity would have flourished in the atmosphere that prevailed among the young during the late sixties and early seventies.

4

STRATEGIES FOR ESTEEM

It is high time that we declare all-out war on the destructive value system I have been describing – the system which reserves self-worth and dignity for a select minority. I reject the notion that inferiority and inadequacy are inevitable, that the present epidemic of self-doubt is unavoidable. Although our task is more difficult for some children than for others, there *are* ways to teach a child of his genuine significance, regardless of the shape of his nose or the size of his ears or the efficiency of his mind. *Every* child is entitled to hold up his head, not in haughtiness and pride, but in confidence and security. This is the concept of human worth intended by our Creator. How foolish for us to doubt our value when He formed us in His own image! His view of the beauty cult was made abundantly clear more than three thousand years ago when Samuel was seeking a king for Israel. Samuel naturally selected the tallest, most handsome son of Jesse, but God told him he had chosen the wrong man, saying:

> Don't judge by a man's face or height, for this [David's brother] is not the one. I don't make decisions the way you do! Men judge by outward appearance, but I look at a man's thoughts and intentions.
>
> (I Samuel 16:7 LIVING BIBLE)

Despite the clarity of this message, we have not taught it to our children. Some of the little folk feel so inferior that they cannot believe even God could love them. They feel so totally worthless and empty, thinking that God neither cares nor understands. Chris was such a child. He wrote the following note to Dr. Richard A. Gardner, a psychotherapist who works with children:

> Dear Docter Gardner
> What is bothering me is that long ago some big person it was a boy about 13 years old. He called me turtle and I know he said that because of my plastic sergery.
> And I think god hates me because of my lip. And when I die he'll probably send me to hell.
>
> Love, Chris

Can't you feel Chris's loneliness and despair? How unfortunate for a seven-year-old child to believe that he is already hated by the entire universe! What a waste of the potential that existed at the moment of his birth. What unnecessary pain he will bear throughout his lifetime. Yet Chris is merely one more victim of a stupid, inane system of evaluating human worth – a system which stresses attributes which cannot be obtained by the majority of our children. Instead of rewarding honesty, integrity, courage, craftsmanship, humour, motherhood, loyalty, patience, diligence, or other virtues which were praised in earlier times, we reserve maximum credit for bright young people who 'look good' on a beach. Isn't it now appropriate that we abandon this needless discrimination?

So what are we to do? How can we, as parents and teachers, build strong egos and indomitable spirits in our children, despite the social forces which prevail? What are the steps necessary to reverse the trend? The suggestions and recommendations which follow are addressed to these questions, offering specific strategies to be applied. These strategies are focused on the early home life, the school years, the adolescent experience and matters pertinent to adults. Each strategy is followed by a question and answer section, reflecting actual requests for specific advice which I have received from parents.

It has been my purpose to formulate a well-defined philosophy – an approach to child rearing – which will contribute to self-esteem from infancy onward.

Strategy No. 1

EXAMINE THE VALUES IN YOUR OWN HOME

In a very real sense, we parents are products of the society whose values I have condemned. We have systematically been taught to worship beauty and brains, as everyone else, and so have our grandmommas and grandpoppas and uncles and aunts and cousins and neighbours. We all want super-children who will amaze the world. Let's face it, folks: we have met the enemy and it is *us*! Often the greatest damage is unintentionally inflicted right in the home, which should be the child's sanctuary and fortress. Furthermore, I have observed in working with parents that their *own* feelings of inferiority make it difficult for them to accept gross imperfections in their children. They don't intend to reject their sons and daughters and they work hard to conceal these inner thoughts. But their 'damaged' child symbolises their own personal inadequacies and failures. Thus, it takes a very mature parent to look down upon an ugly child, or one who is clearly deficient in mentality, saying, 'Not only do I love you, little one, but I recognise your immeasurable worth as a human being.'

The first step in building your child's esteem, then, is to examine your own feelings – even being willing to expose those guilt-laden attitudes which may have been unconscious, heretofore. Are you secretly disappointed because your child is so ordinary? Have you rejected him, at times, because of his lack of appeal and charm? Do you think he is dumb and stupid? Was he born during a difficult time, imposing financial and physical stress on the family? Did you want a girl instead of a boy? Or a boy instead of a girl? Was this child conceived out of wedlock, forcing an unwanted marriage? Do you resent the freedom you lost when he came, or the demands he places on your time and effort? Does he embarrass you by being either too loud and rambunctious or too inward and withdrawn? Quite obviously, you can't teach a child to respect himself when you dislike him for reasons of your own! By examining your innermost feelings, perhaps with the help of an understanding counsellor or doctor, you *can* make room in your heart as a loving parent for your less-than-perfect youngster. After all, what right do we have to demand superchildren when we are so ordinary ourselves?!

A sizeable proportion of your child's self-concept emerges from the way he thinks you 'see' him. He watches what you say and do with interest. He is more alert to your 'statements' regarding his worth than any other subject, even reading your unspoken (and perhaps unconscious) attitudes. Dr. Stanley Coopersmith conducted an exhaustive study of self-esteem (described more fully in Strategy No. 6) and concluded that parents have a tremendous influence on their child's view of himself. They can either equip him with the confidence necessary to withstand the social pressures I have described, or they can leave him virtually defenceless. The difference is in the quality of their interaction. When the child is convinced that he is greatly loved and respected by his parents, he is inclined to accept his own worth as a person.

However, I have observed that many children know intuitively that they are loved by their parents, but they do not believe they are held in high esteem by them. These seemingly contradictory attitudes are not so uncommon in human relationships. A wife can love her alcoholic husband, for example, yet disrespect him for what he has become. Thus, a child can conclude in his own mind, 'Sure they love me because I'm their child – I can see that I'm important to them – but they are not proud of me as a person. I'm a disappointment to them. I've let them down. I didn't turn out like they had hoped.'

At the risk of being redundant, I must emphasise the point

made above: it is very easy to convey love and disrespect at the same time. A child can know that you would actually give your life for him, if required, and yet your doubts about his acceptability show through. You are tense and nervous when he starts to speak to guests or outsiders. You butt in to explain what he was trying to say or laugh nervously when his remarks sound foolish. When someone asks him a direct question, you interrupt and answer for him. You reveal your frustration when you are trying to comb his hair or make him 'look nice' for an important event. He knows you think it is an impossible assignment. If he is to spend a weekend away from the family, you give him an extended lecture on how to avoid making a fool of himself. These subtle behaviours are signals to the child that you don't trust him with *your* image – that he must be supervised closely to avoid embarrassing the whole family. He reads disrespect in your manner, though it is framed in genuine love. The love is a private thing between you – whereas confidence and admiration are 'other' oriented, having social implications to those outside the family.

Loving your child, therefore, is only half of the task of building self-esteem. The element of respect must be added if you are to counterbalance the insults which society will later throw at him. Unless *somebody* believes in his worth, the world can be a cold and lonely place, indeed. It is for this reason that I described the enormous threats to esteem in the last two chapters. I have wanted each parent to see just what his child faces in life and the vital importance of preparing him to meet his critics head on.

There are, I believe, five common barriers which can cause your child to doubt his worth, even when he is deeply loved. I would suggest that the reader examine his own home as we discuss these pitfalls to be avoided.

(1) *Parental Insensitivity*. If there is one lesson parents need to learn most urgently, it is to guard what they say in the presence of their children. How many times, following a speaking engagement, have I been consulted by a parent regarding a particular problem her child is having. As Mom

describes the gritty details, I notice that the object of all this conversation is standing about a yard behind her. His ears are ten feet tall as he listens to a candid description of all his faults. I visibly flinch when I hear a parent unintentionally disassemble esteem in this fashion. Just this afternoon, for example, I took my son and daughter to a park during a break in my writing schedule. While there, an insensitive mother was talking to me about her six-year-old boy, Roger, who stood within hearing distance just a few feet away.

She spoke in Gatling-gun fashion: 'He had a high fever when he was born, about 105, at least. The doctor couldn't do nothing to help him. He gave Roger the wrong kind of pills. Now Roger won't ever be the same. They say he has some brain damage now, and he don't learn too good in school.'

If Roger were my boy, his mental handicap would be the very last thing I would let him hear me describe to a stranger. It was like saying, 'This is my son, Roger. He's the dumb one – you know, there's something wrong with his brain.' How imperceptive she was of her unfortunate son. Roger did not show shock. In fact, he didn't even look up. But you can bet he heard his mother, and his self-concept will *always* reflect what she said.

Surprisingly, it is not just insensitive parents who blunder into this kind of foolishness. I recently referred a bright nine-year-old boy to a neurologist because of severe learning problems. After giving the lad a thorough examination, the physician called in his parents and discussed the full details of the boy's 'brain damage' in front of his wide-eyed little patient. How can we preserve self-esteem when we have totally lost touch with childhood ourselves? Don't we know they are listening to us? It is a wise adult who understands that self-esteem is the most fragile characteristic in human nature, and once broken, its reconstruction is more difficult than repairing Humpty Dumpty.

Parental sensitivity should be especially sharp in regard to matters pertaining to physical attractiveness and intelligence. Those are the two main 'soft spots' where their children are most vulnerable. It is, of course, impossible to shut out this value system entirely, for it penetrates like termites through the walls. Consider how the importance of beauty is taught through the casual occurrences and conversations of each day:

Advertisements: 'You, too, can have gorgeous hair.'

Mother: 'Mr. and Mrs. Martin sure have cute kids, don't they?'

Father: 'When are you going to start growing, Billy?'

Fairy Stories: 'Then the ugly duckling sat down to cry.'

Television: 'The *new* Miss America is . . .'

Relative: 'My, what a pretty little girl you've become.'

The whole world seems organised to convey this one message to the younger set. While you can't shield your child from its impact, you don't have to add to it yourself. You can also screen out the television programmes which are most offensive and help your child select good reading material.

Sensitivity is a vitally important skill for teachers as well. Dr. Clyde Narramore, author and psychologist, describes being in a classroom where a teacher wanted to convey the concepts of 'small' versus 'large'. She selected the tiniest little runt in the room, a withdrawn fellow who rarely made a sound, and instructed him to stand beside her at the front. 'Small!' she said. 'David is small.' She then dismissed him and summoned the tallest girl in the class. 'Large! Large! Sharon is very large!' said the teacher. Dr. Narramore said every child in the room could see David and Sharon blush in humiliation, but the teacher failed to notice. We cannot preserve the esteem of the next generation if our eyes are always aimed about twenty-four inches above their bowed heads.

Sensitivity is the key word. It means 'tuning in' to the thoughts and feelings of our kids, listening to the cues they give us and reacting appropriately to what we detect there.

(2) *Fatigue and Time Pressure.* Why do dedicated parents have to be reminded to be sensitive to the needs of their children, anyway? Shouldn't this be the natural expression of

their love and concern? Yes it should, but Mom and Dad have some problems of their own. They are pushed to the limits of their endurance by the pressure of time. Dad is holding down three jobs and he huffs and puffs to keep up with it all. Mom never has a free minute, either. Tomorrow night, for example, she is having eight guests for dinner and she only has this one evening to clean the house, go to the market, arrange the flowers for the centrepiece, and put the hem in the dress she will wear. Her 'to do' list is three pages long and she already has a splitting headache from it all. She opens a can of 'Spaghetti-Os' for the kids' supper and hopes the troops will stay out of her hair. About 7 p.m., little Larry tracks down his perspiring mother and says, 'Look what I just drawed, Mom.' She glances downward and says, 'Uh huh,' obviously thinking about something else.

Ten minutes later, Larry asks her to get him some juice. She complies but resents his intrusion. She is behind schedule and her tension is mounting. Five minutes later he interrupts again, this time wanting her to reach a toy that sits on the top shelf of the closet. She stands looking down at him for a moment and then hurries down the hall to meet his demand, mumbling as she goes. But as she passes his bedroom door, she notices that he has spread his toys all over the floor and made a mess with the glue. Mom explodes. She screams and threatens and shakes Larry till his teeth rattle.

Does this drama sound familiar? It should, for 'routine panic' is becoming an American way of life. I recently conducted an inquiry among seventy-five middle-class married women, between twenty-five and thirty-five years of age. I asked them to indicate the sources of depression which most often send them into despair and gloom. Many common problems were revealed, including in-law conflicts, financial hardships, difficulties with children, sexual problems, and mood fluctuations associated with menstrual and physiological distress. But to my surprise, *fatigue and time pressure* was tagged as *the* most troublesome source of depression by half the group; the other half ranked it a close second! It is obvious that many families live on this kind of last-minute, emergency schedule, making it impossible to meet the demands of their own overcommitments. Why do they do it? The women whom I surveyed admitted their dislike for the pace they kept, yet it has become a monster which defies containment. Faster and faster they run, jamming more and more activities into their hectic days. Even their recreation is marked by the same breakneck pace. There was a time when a man didn't fret if he missed a stage coach; he'd just catch it next month. Now if a fellow misses a section of a revolving door he's thrown into despair!

But guess who is the inevitable loser from this breathless lifestyle? It's the little guy who is leaning against the wall with his hands in the pockets of his blue jeans. He misses his father during the long day and tags around after him at night, saying, 'Play ball, Dad!' But Dad is pooped. Besides, he has a briefcase full of work to be done. Mom had promised to take him to the park this afternoon, but then she had to go to that Women's Auxiliary meeting at the last minute. The lad gets the message – his folks are busy again. So he drifts into the family room and watches two hours of pointless cartoons and reruns on television.

Children just don't fit into a 'to do' list very well. It takes time to be an effective parent when children are small. It takes time to introduce them to good books – it takes time to fly kites and play punch ball and put together jigsaw puzzles. it takes time to listen, once more, to the skinned-knee episode and talk about the bird with the broken wing. These are the building blocks of esteem, held together with the mortar of love. But they seldom materialise amidst busy timetables. Instead, crowded lives produce fatigue – and fatigue produces irritability – and irritability produces indifference – and indifference can be interpreted by the child as a lack of genuine affection and personal esteem.

As the commercial says, 'Slow down, America!' What is your rush, anyway? Don't you know your children will be gone so quickly and you will have nothing but blurred memories of those years when they needed you? I'm not suggesting that we invest our entire adult lives into the next generation, nor must everyone become parents. But once those children are here, they had better fit into our schedule somewhere. This is, however, a lonely message at the present time in our society. Others are telling Mom to go to work – have a career – do her own thing – turn her babies over to employees of the state working in child-care centres. Let someone else discipline, teach, and guide her toddler. While she's at it, though, she'd better hope that her 'someone else' gets across the message of esteem and worth to that pudgy little butterball who waves 'goodbye' to his mommy each morning.

(3) *Guilt*. In case you haven't noticed, parenthood is a very guilt-producing affair – even for the dedicated 'professional'. The conflict of interest between the needs of children and the demands of adult responsibilities, as described above, is only one of many inconsistencies which can strike pangs of guilt in our hearts. (It is interesting to me that the situation gradually reverses itself as we age, with our grown-up children then feeling guilty over their failures with us!) Since no one can do the job perfectly, we subject ourselves to a constant cross-examination in the courtroom of parental acceptability. Was I fair in my discipline? Did I overreact out of frustration and anger? Have I been partial to the child who is my favourite? Did I cause that illness by giving him poor care? Was the accident my fault? Have I made the same mistakes for which I resented my own parents? Round and round go the self-doubts and recriminations.

I have even seen parents agonise over circumstances totally beyond their control, such as when they give birth to a mentally retarded child. Although the cause of the child's defect was genetic and completely unknowable until it occurred, they often interpret the disaster as punishment for some past sin. Once that idea has been accepted as truth, they will bear the personal responsibility for their child's misfortune from that day forward. This unfounded guilt can drive a wedge between two happily married people, destroying their relationship and consuming them in bitterness.

Guilt can interfere with a healthy parent-child relationship in numerous ways. First, it can take the joy out of parenthood, turning the entire responsibility into a painful chore. Secondly, guilt almost always affects the way a parent handles a child; the typical reaction is to buy everything Junior screams for, whether he needs it or not, and to become much too permissive in matters of control. The reasoning seems to be, 'With all that I have done wrong, the least I can do for the child is avoid punishment and unpleasantness.' As we will discuss later, self-esteem splinters under that free-wheeling environment. Thirdly, through some mystery of perception, a child can usually 'feel' hidden guilt in his parents. He knows something unidentifiable is there, and wonders about its meaning. He may well conclude that it is all his fault. In short, guilt can be another formidable barrier in building self-respect among the young.

The best way to handle guilt is to face it squarely, using it as a source of motivation for change, where warranted. Dr. William Glasser said, and I agree, that guilt is a valuable emotion, providing the energy to improve and grow. Thus, I would suggest that guilty parents sit down together and discuss their personal dissatisfaction. They should actually write down their most troubling parental shortcomings. Each item should then be assessed as follows: Is my guilt valid? Can I do anything about it? If so, how? If not, isn't it appropriate that I lay the matter to rest?

Remember, again, that none of us can be perfect parents, any more than we can be perfect human beings. We get tired and frustrated and disappointed and irritable, affecting the way we approach those little fellows around our feet. But fortunately, we are permitted to make many mistakes through the years – provided the overall tone is somewhere near the right note.

(4) *Rivals for Love.* My son arrived on the scene when his sister was five years of age. She had been the only granddaughter on either side of the family and had received all the adult attention that can be heaped upon a child. Then suddenly, her secure kingdom was invaded by a cute little

fellow who captured and held the centre stage. All of the relatives cuddled, cooed, rocked, bounced, and hugged baby Ryan, while Danae watched suspiciously from the wings. As we drove home from Grandmother's house on a Sunday afternoon, about a week after Ryan's arrival, my daughter suddenly said, 'Daddy, you know I'm just talking. You know, I don't mean to be bad or anything, but sometimes I wish little Ryan wasn't here!'

She had given us a valuable clue to her feelings in that brief sentence, and we immediately seized the opportunity she had provided. We moved her into the front seat of the car so we could discuss what she had said. We told her we understood how she felt and assured her of our love. We also explained that a baby is completely helpless and will die if people don't take care of him – feed, clothe, change, and love him. We reminded her that she was taken care of that way when she was a baby, and explained that Ryan would soon grow up too. We were also careful in the months that followed to minimise the threat to her place in our hearts. By giving careful attention to her feelings and security, the relationship with her brother developed into a lasting friendship and love.

Danae's admission was not a typical response among children. Much more commonly, a child will be unable or unwilling to express the insecurity brought by a newborn rival, requiring his parents to read more subtle signs and cues. The most reliable symptom of the I've-been-replaced syndrome is a sudden return to infantile behaviour. Obviously, 'If babyhood is where it's at, then I'll be a baby again.' Therefore, the child throws temper tantrums, wets the bed, sucks his thumb, holds tightly to Mamma, baby talks, etc. In this situation, the child has observed a clear and present danger and is solving it in the best way he knows.

If your firstborn child seems to feel like a has-been, I would suggest the following procedures be implemented:

(1) Bring his feelings out in the open and help him verbalise them. When a child is acting silly in front

of adults, trying to make them laugh or notice him, it is good to take him in your arms and say, 'What's the matter, Joey? Do you need some attention today?' Gradually, a child can be taught to use similar words when he feels excluded or rejected. 'I need some attention, Dad. Will you play with me?' By verbalising his feelings, you also help him to understand himself better.

(2) Don't let antisocial behaviour succeed. If the child cries when the baby-sitter arrives, leave him anyway. A temper tantrum can be greeted with a firm swat, etc. However, reveal little anger and displeasure, remembering that the entire episode is motivated by a threat to your love.

(3) Meet his needs in ways that grant status to him for being older. Take him to the park, making it clear that the baby is too little to go; talk 'up' to him about the things he can do that the baby can't – he can use the bathroom instead of his pants, for example. Let him help take care of the baby so he will feel he is part of the family process.

It is not difficult to convey love to more than one child simultaneously provided you put your mind (and heart) to it.

This first strategy, in summary, involves examining the emotional content of your home. Does it contribute to self-confidence or self-degradation? Does it meet the basic emotional needs or does it leave them unsatisfied and yearning? Does it reserve respect and admiration for the bright and beautiful superchild, or does it grant human worth to every person on this earth? Does it reinforce the best in life, or the worst? Someday, when your little one is grown, he will look back in anger or appreciation, depending on the answers to those relevant questions.

Questions and Answers

(1) *What about good-natured teasing and joking within the family? Is it harmful to laugh and kid each other?*

The most healthy families are those which can laugh together, and I certainly don't think our egos should be so fragile that we all have to walk on cracked eggs around each other. However, even innocent humour can be painful when one child is always the object of the jokes. When one youngster has an embarrassing feature, such as bed-wetting or thumb-sucking or stuttering or a striking physical flaw, the other members of the family should be encouraged to tread softly on the exposed nerves thereabout. And particularly, one should not ridicule a child for his size, whether he is a small boy or a large girl. There is nothing funny about that subject. This is the guiding principle: it is wise not to tease a child about the features he is also defending outside the home. And when he asks for any joke to end, his wishes should be honoured.

(2) *Must I praise my child all day for every little thing he does? Isn't it possible to create a spoiled brat by telling him his every move is wonderful?*

Yes, inflationary praise is unnecessary. Junior quickly catches on to your verbal game, and your words then lose their meaning. It is helpful to distinguish between the concepts of *flattery* vs. *praise*. Flattery is unearned. It is what Grandma says when she comes for a visit: 'Oh, look at my beautiful little girl! You're getting prettier each day. I'll bet you'll have to beat the boys off with a club when you get to be a teenager!' Or, 'My, what a smart boy you are.' Flattery occurs when you heap compliments upon the child for something he did not achieve.

Praise, on the other hand, is used to reinforce positive, constructive behaviour. It should be highly specific rather than general. 'You've been a good boy . . .' is unsatisfactory.

'I like the way you kept your room straight today,' is better. Parents should always watch for opportunities to offer genuine, well-deserved praise to their children, while avoiding empty flattery.

(3) *We live in 'routine panic' in our home, as you described. I have three children under six, and I never catch up with my work. How can I slow down when it takes every minute of the day (and night) to care for my children?*

There may be a helpful answer in the way you spend your money. Most Americans maintain a 'priority list' of things to purchase when enough money has been saved for that purpose. They plan ahead to reupholster the sofa or carpet the dining-room floor or buy a newer car. However, it is my conviction that domestic help for the mother of small children should appear on that priority list too. Without it, she is sentenced to the same responsibility day in and day out, seven days a week. For several years, she is unable to escape the unending burden of dirty nappies, runny noses, and unwashed dishes. It is my belief that she will do a more efficient job in those tasks and be a better mother if she can share the load with someone else occasionally. More explicitly, I feel she should get out of the house completely for one day a week, doing something for sheer enjoyment. This seems more important to the happiness of the home than buying new curtains or a power saw for Dad.

But how can middle-class families afford housecleaning and baby-sitting services in these inflationary days? It can best be accomplished by using competent high-school students instead of older adults. I would suggest that a call be placed to the counselling office of the nearest senior high school. Tell the counsellor that you need a mature, third-year student to do some cleaning. Do not reveal that you're looking for a regular employee. When the referred girl arrives, try her out for a day and see how she handles responsibility. If she's very efficient, offer her a weekly job. If she is slow and flighty, thank her for coming and call for another student the following week. There is a remarkable difference in maturity level between high-school girls, and you'll eventually find one who works like an adult.

Incidentally, if your husband is saving for that new power saw, it might be better to eliminate one of your own priority items first time around. Either way, don't tell him I sent you.

(4) *I am very disappointed with the way my four-year-old is turning out. If the present trends continue, he will be a failure as an adult. Is it possible to 'forecast' a child's future character and personality traits from this early age?*

Rene Voeltzel said, 'We must not look too soon in the child for the person he will later become.' It is unfair and damaging to judge him too soon. Be patient and give your little fellow time to mature. Work gently on the traits that concern you the most but, by all means, allow him the privilege of being a child. He will be one for such a brief moment, anyway.

Strategy No. 2
RESERVE ADOLESCENCE FOR THE ADOLESCENTS

In recent years, toy manufacturers and other business interests have been successful in changing the nature of children's play. Instead of three- and four-year-old boys and girls playing with stuffed animals, balls, cars, trucks, model horses, and the traditional memorabilia of childhood, they are now learning to fantasise about life as an adolescent. The most influential force behind this trend has been the Barbie-Doll movement, and I am unalterably opposed to the entire concept! There could be no better method for teaching the worship of beauty and materialism than is done with luscious Barbie. If we intentionally sought to drill our babies on the necessity of growing up rich and gorgeous, we could do no better than has already been done. Did you ever see an ugly Barbie Doll? Has she ever had even the slightest imperfection? Of course not! She oozes femininity and sex appeal. Her hair is thick and gleaming – loaded with 'body' (whatever in the world that is). Her long, thin legs, curvaceous bust, and delicate feet are absolutely perfect. Her airbrushed skin is without flaw or blemish (except for a little statement on her bottom that she was 'Made in Japan'). She never gets pimples or blackheads, and there is not an ounce of fat on her pink body. Not only is Barbie one of the beautiful people, but so are all her buddies. Her swinging boyfriend, Ken, is an adolescent composite of Charles Atlas, Rock Hudson, and Clark Kent (mild-mannered reporter for the *Daily Planet*). These idealised models load an emotional time bomb set to explode the moment a real live thirteen-year-old takes her first long look in the mirror. No doubt about it – Barbie she ain't!

Yet it is not the physical perfection of these Barbie Dolls (and her many competitors) that concerns me most; of much greater harm are the teenage games that they inspire. Ken and Barbie go on dates, learn to dance, drive sports cars, get suntans, take camping trips, exchange marriage vows, and have babies (hopefully in that order). The entire adolescent culture with its emphasis on sexual awareness is illustrated to tiny little girls who ought to be thinking about more childish things. This places our children on an unnatural timetable likely to reach the peak of sexual interest several years before it is due – with all the obvious implications for their social and emotional health.

We not only teach our small children about adolescent values through their toys, but we hit 'em with an effective one-two punch! Television, particularly the Saturday morning variety, is loaded with teenage trivia. Seemingly innocent programmes, such as Archie and his pals, are focused exclusively on the adolescent experience. By the time a child is six years old, he has spent thousands of hours before the great tube, learning the values, attitudes, dress, behaviour, and thrills of those days to come. Teenage stars are carefully created and marketed to the preteen set, which responds with appropriate crushes and fan mail. All of this accounts, in part, for the trend towards younger and younger dating and sexual awareness.

I believe it is desirable to postpone the adolescent experience until it is summoned by the happy hormones. Therefore, I strongly recommend that parents screen the influences to which their children will be exposed, keeping activities appropriate for each age. And *anything* which tells your child he must be beautiful and rich should be viewed with suspicion. While we cannot isolate our small children from the world as it is, we don't have to turn our babies into teenyboppers.

Questions and Answers

(1) *Do you think children between five and ten should be allowed to listen to rock music on the radio?*

Not if it can be prevented gracefully. Here again, rock music is an expression of an adolescent culture. The words of teenagers' songs deal with dating, broken hearts, drug usage, and luv-luv-luv. This is just what you don't want your seven-year-old thinking about. Instead, his world of excitement should consist of adventure books, Disney-type productions, and family activities – camping, fishing, sporting events, games, etc.

On the other hand, it is unwise to appear dictatorial and oppressive in such matters. I would suggest that you keep your preteen so involved with wholesome activities that he does not need to dream of the days to come.

(2) *You mentioned the names of some television programmes which are harmful. What is your view of T.V., generally? Should parents attempt to regulate what their children watch?*

I have some serious concerns about television's impact on our society, and particularly on our younger generation. According to Dr. Gerald Looney, University of Arizona, by the time the average preschool child reaches fourteen years of age, he will have witnessed 18,000 murders on T.V., and

countless hours of related violence, nonsense, and unadulter-
ated drivel! Dr. Saul Kapel states, furthermore, that the most
time-consuming activity in the life of a child is neither school
nor family interaction. It is television, absorbing 14,000
valuable hours during the course of childhood! That is equivalent to sitting before the tube eight hours a day, con-
tinuously for 4.9 years!

There are other aspects of television which demand its
regulation and controls. For one thing, it is an enemy of
communication within the family. How can we talk to each
other when a million-dollar production in living colour is
always beckoning our attention? I am also concerned about
the current fashion whereby each programme director is
compelled to include all the avant-garde ideas – go a little
farther – use a little more profanity – discuss the undis-
cussable – assault the public concept of good taste and
decency. In so doing, they are hacking away at the foun-
dations of the family and all that represents the Christian
ethic. In recent seasons, for example, we were offered
hilariously funny episodes involving abortion, divorce,
extramarital relationships, rape, and the ever-popular
theme, 'Father is an idiot.' If this is 'social relevance,' then I
am sick unto death of the messages I have been fed.

The television actress Sally Field was interviewed by
Marilyn Beck of the *Kansas City Star*, September 9, 1973.
Following are Miss Field's candid views of her then-new
television show.

'They had me playing a twenty-three-year-old virgin, and
I couldn't perpetuate that kind of fraud. It simply isn't
today. . . .' Miss Field's objections were honoured by the
producer and the thrust of the show made saucier. 'For
instance,' she stated, 'in the opening segment you'll see John
and me on our first date. He drops me off at my apartment
and before he has a chance to ask, I tell him I know what he's
thinking and he can't come upstairs – but I explain that the
reason he can't is because my roommate is home. In other
words, I want it obvious to viewers that this is a character
with real emotions. She isn't turning her date off because

she's one of those outmoded "no-no" types. She's as tempted as he is. She digs him – but they're going to have to wait a while.'

My response towards this kind of 'relevance' can only be described as one of utter disgust. Did you catch the tender scene? The swinging Sally and her hungry boyfriend were on their *first* date, yet she needed an excuse (the bedroom is occupied) in order to postpone sexual intercourse for 'a while'. Bless her sensitive little heart, she wouldn't want John-John to think she was an outmoded 'no-no' type. That would be unthinkable. It is my guess that John won't have to wait too long to deal with Sally's 'real emotions'. Perhaps five million impressionable adolescents will watch that programme, each comparing his mores with those of the very modern Miss Field. With great certainty I can say that my home will not be represented among the viewers!

Television, with its unparalleled capacity for teaching and edifying, has occasionally demonstrated the potential it carries. 'Little House on the Prairie' is, I believe, the best programme now available for young children. I would not, therefore, recommend smashing the television set in despair. Rather, we must learn to control it instead of becoming its slave. My children are permitted to watch one hour of cartoons on Saturday morning, and a one-half hour programme each afternoon, selected from an approved list. This policy is flexible if special programmes of interest are televised. By this kind of close supervision, we can derive the benefits offered by the tube without allowing it to dominate our lives.

It is my opinion that the mother who plants her impressionable preschool child in front of the television set for the sake of her own convenience is making a mistake with irrevocable consequences!

Strategy No. 3

TEACH YOUR CHILD A 'NO-KNOCK' POLICY

One of the most obvious characteristics of a person who feels inferior is that he talks about his deficiencies to anyone who will listen. A fat person feels compelled to apologise to his companions for ordering a hot-fudge sundae. He echoes what he imagines they're thinking: 'I'm already fat enough without eating this,' he says, scooping up the cherry and syrup with his spoon. Likewise, a woman who thinks she's dumb will admit freely, 'I am really bad at maths; I can hardly add two and two.' This kind of self-denigration is not as uncommon as one might think. Listen to yourself in the weeks that come. You might be surprised by how often you emphasise your faults to your friends.

While there is no virtue in becoming an image-conscious phoney, trying to be something we're not, I believe it is also a mistake to go to the other extreme. While you are blabbing about all of your ridiculous inadequacies, the listener is formulating his impression of you. He will later 'see' you and treat you according to the evidence you've provided. After all, you're the expert on that subject. Furthermore, having put your feelings into words, they become solidified as fact in your own mind.

Therefore, we should teach a 'no-knock' policy to our children. They should learn that constant self-criticism can become a bad habit, and it accomplishes nothing. There is a big difference between accepting blame when it is valid and in simply chattering about one's inferiority. This might be a difficult distinction for your children to grasp, although you can get excellent help from the 'Peanuts' comic strip. Charlie Brown is so perceptive of his own inferiority that he worries about it out loud to all his friends. Lucy, the sweetheart, then smashes him over the head with the information he provided. (This cartoon appears on page 84.)

What a wonderful memory of childhood Charles Schulz, the 'Peanuts' creator, has shown. The phenomenal success of his cartoon is based on his recollection of humiliation in school, unbearable blunders, and feelings of failure. We laugh because he hits so close to home. You have stood in Charlie Brown's lonesome shoes, and so have I. When I was in the third grade, I was playing left field in a hotly contested baseball game. How clearly I remember that black day.

Willie Mays was up to bat and he hit a routine fly ball – a simple little pop fly – and all I had to do was catch it. But there in front of five million fans, mostly girls, I let the ball drop right through my outstretched fingers. In fact, it jammed my thumb on its way to the ground. I can still hear the pounding feet of four base runners heading for home plate. In desperation, I grabbed the ball and threw it to the umpire, who stepped aside and let it roll at least a city block. *Booo!* yelled half of the five million hostile fans. *Yeaaa!* yelled the other half. I bled and died right out there in the left field that afternoon. It was a lonely funeral; I was the only mourner. After careful deliberation in the days that followed, I gave up baseball and have seldom played since. I've enjoyed basketball, tennis, track, and other assorted sports activities, but baseball and I parted company on that afternoon. Charlie Brown, who also takes himself too seriously, might well consider the same course of action. And by all means, he should keep his 'failures' to himself. If he'd close his big mouth, people might not even notice – they are, as you know, thinking about themselves anyway.

Questions and Answers

(1) *What do children most often dislike about themselves?*

In an important study by E. A. Douvan, titled *Adolescent Girls*, nearly 2,000 girls from eleven to eighteen years of age were asked, 'What would you most like to change about yourself if you could . . . your looks, your personality, or your life?' Fifty-nine percent mentioned some aspect of their physical appearance. (Only four percent desired greater ability.) The most common personal dissatisfaction for both boys and girls concerns facial defects, primarily skin problems. In a later study by H. V. Cobb, children in grades four to fourteen were asked to complete the sentence, 'I wish I were': The majority of the boys answered 'taller' and the girls answered 'smaller'. Certainly, there is a great volume of scientific evidence to document children's preoccupation and dissatisfaction with their own physical characteristics.

(2) *My child is often ridiculed and hurt by the other children on our block, and I don't know how to handle the situation. He gets very depressed and comes home crying frequently. How should I respond when this happens?*

When your child has been rejected in this manner, he is badly in need of a friend – and you are elected. Let him talk. Don't try to tell him that it doesn't hurt or that it's silly to be so sensitive. Ask him if he knows what it is that his 'friends' don't like. (He may be causing their reaction by dominance, selfishness, or dishonesty.) Be understanding and sympathetic without weeping in mutual despair. As soon as appropriate, involve yourself with him in a game or some other activity which he will enjoy. And finally, set about resolving the underlying cause.

I would suggest that you ask your child to invite one of his school friends to go to the zoo on Saturday (or offer other attractive 'bait') and then spend the night at your house. Genuine friendship often grows from such beginnings. Even the hostile children on the block may be more kind when only one of them is invited at a time. Not only can you help your child make friends in this way, but you can observe the social mistakes he is making to drive them away. The information you gain can later be used to help him improve his relationship with others.

(3) *My ten-year-old daughter hates to have her hair in a pigtail because her friends don't wear theirs that way. I have always loved pigtails, ever since I was a little girl. Am I wrong to make her please me by wearing her hair the way I want it?*

Yes, particularly if your daughter feels unnecessarily different and foolish with her friends. Social pressure on the nonconformist is severe, and you should not place your daughter in this uncomfortable position. Closeness between generations comes from the child's knowledge that his parent understands and appreciates his feelings. Your inflexibility on this point reveals a lack of empathy and may bring later resentment.

Strategy No. 4

HELP YOUR CHILD TO COMPENSATE

Now let's get down to the nitty-gritty. Some children have much greater handicaps than others and are almost certainly destined for emotional trouble during adolescence. Their anxious parents can see it coming like a gathering storm, even prior to the school years. Perhaps a child is particularly ugly or he might have a severe learning problem. For whatever reason, everybody can see that he is going to get clobbered by life. What are his parents to do? What are you to do in preparing your child to confront a most unsympathetic world?

First we must be realistic. There are no simple 'cures' which will eliminate the struggle, short of changing the values of an entire society. Other books on self-esteem naïvely assert that parental love, if vigorously expressed every day, is all that a child needs to develop self-confidence. I wish that were true, but in fact, a child's view of himself is a product of two important influences: (1) the quality of his home life; (2) his social experiences outside the family. The first of these forces is much easier to control than the second. There is no emotional armour which will make your child impervious to rejection and ridicule in his social contacts. It will always hurt to be laughed at, snubbed, ignored, or attacked by others. But I would remind you at this point that the human personality grows through mild adversity, *provided it is not crushed in the process*. Contrary to what you might believe, the ideal environment for your child is not one devoid of problems and trials. I would not, even if I could, sweep aside every hurdle from the paths of my children, leaving them to glide along in mirth. They deserve the right to face problems and profit from the confrontation.

I have verified the value of minor stress from my own experience. My childhood was remarkably happy and care-free. I was loved beyond any doubt, and my academic performance was never a cause for discomfort. In fact, I have enjoyed happiness and fulfillment thus far in my entire life-time, with the exception of two painful years. Those stressful days occurred during my seventh and eighth grade days, lasting through ages thirteen and fourteen. During this period of time, I found myself in a social crossfire, giving rise to the same intense feelings of inferiority and self-doubt I have described herein. As strange as it seems, however, these two years have contributed more positive features to my adult personality than any other span of which I am aware. My empathy for others, my desire to succeed in life, my motivation in graduate school, my understanding of in-feriority, and my communication with teenagers are primarily the products of an agitated adolescence. Who would have thought anything useful could have come from those twenty-four months? Yet the discomfort proved to be a valuable instructor in this instance.

Though it is hard to accept at the time, your child also needs the minor setbacks and disappointments which come his way. How can he learn to cope with problems and frustration if his early experiences are totally without trial? A tree which is planted in a rain forest is never forced to extend its roots downward in search of water; consequently it remains poorly anchored and can be toppled by a moderate wind storm. By contrast, a mesquite tree planted in a dry desert is threatened by its hostile environment. It can only survive by sending its roots more than thirty feet deep into the earth, seeking cool water. But through its adaptation to the arid land, something else happens. The well-rooted tree becomes strong and steady against all assailants. This illustration applies to our children, as well: those who have learned to conquer their problems are more secure than those who have never faced them. Our task as parents, then, is not to eliminate every challenge for our children; it is to serve as a confident ally on their behalf, encouraging when they are distressed, intervening when the threats are over-whelming, and above all, giving them the tools with which to overcome the obstacles.

One of those vital tools involves a process called *compensation*. It means the individual counterbalances his weak-nesses by capitalising on his strengths. It is our job as parents to help our children find those strengths and learn to exploit them for all the self-satisfaction they will yield. And this brings us to a very important concept to be grasped: in-feriority can either crush and paralyse an individual, or it can provide tremendous emotional energy which powers every kind of success and achievement. Where do you suppose the former world's champion chess player, Bobby Fischer, got the drive and ambition to read chess, play chess, think chess, and dream chess twenty-four hours a day? Merv Griffin asked him that question on his television show. 'It was some people thinking maybe I wasn't as good as they were when I was a kid,' Fischer replied.

Where do you think the great writer Thomas Wolfe derived the energy and stamina to sit at a typewriter for eighteen or twenty hours a day, months at a time? What pushes a distance runner to plod along for thirty miles in the lonely sand before the sun rises each morning? What inner need propels a student into the rigours of medical school, pushing himself to the limits of his endurance for four years of mental discipline? The power behind these and other kinds of success almost invariably springs from the need for self-worth – the need to prove something about one's adequacy – the need to *compensate*!

Will your child collapse under the weight of inferiority, or will he use it to supercharge his initiative and drive? Will he 'hide' or 'seek'? The answer will probably depend on the availability of compensatory skills. And, I repeat, it is your job as a parent to help him find them. Perhaps he can establish his niche in music – many children do. Maybe he can develop his artistic talent or learn to write or cultivate mechanical skills or build model airplanes or raise rabbits for fun and profit. Regardless of what the choice is, the key is to start him down that road early. There is nothing more risky than sending a teenager into the storms of adolescence with no skills, no unique knowledge, no means of compensating. When this occurs, his ego is stark naked. He cannot say, 'I may not be the most popular student in school, but I am the best trumpet player in the band!' His only source of self-esteem comes from the acceptance of other students — and their love is notoriously fickle.

Is compensation an alternative only for those children who are particularly gifted in an area? Certainly not. There is something emotionally satisfying for nearly everyone, if the person can find it. I saw this process in operation even among those of very meagre ability when I was working at Pacific State Hospital for the Mentally Retarded, in Pomona, California. Every afternoon, for example, I heard a blaring trombone concert coming from a nearby hillside, playing something vaguely recognisable as John Philip Sousa marches. I had no idea who was responsible for the serenades.

Then one day as I walked across the grounds of the hospital, a patient about seventeen years old ran up to me and said: 'Hi. My name is James Walter Jackson (not his real name) and I'm the fellow who plays the trombone. Now I need your help to get a message through to Santa Claus, because I've gotta have a new trombone. The one I have is all beat up and I want a brand new, silver Olds, with purple velvet lining in the case. Will you tell him that for me?'

Well, I was a bit taken aback, but I volunteered to do what I could. That afternoon as I discussed James Walter Jackson with another staff member, he gave me a little background on the message to Santa. The year before, this patient had told several people that he would like Santa Claus to bring him a trombone. One of the hospital workers had an old instrument in his garage which had about seen its day, so on Christmas morning, it was donated to James Walter Jackson with credit given to Santa.

James was delighted, of course, but he was a bit disappointed by all those bumps and dings. He figured he hadn't been specific enough in his prior message to Santa, so he would do better next time. He launched a year-long campaign designed to let the North Pole know exactly what he had in mind. He stopped everyone he met on the street and told them precisely what to tell Santa.

Shortly after that, I saw James Walter Jackson for the last time. I was driving my car out of the hospital grounds when I noticed this amicable patient in the rearview mirror. He was running down the road behind my car, waving for me to stop. I pulled to the curb and let him catch up with me; he put his head in the window and said, panting, 'Don't forget to tell him that I want the long-lasting kind!' I hope someone bought James Walter Jackson what he wanted so badly. His ability to compensate depended on it.

Without question, the richest harvest of compensation in the adolescent world can be found in the area of athletics. This has long been true for boys, and it is becoming more applicable for girls, as well. Referring back to the Charlie Brown comic, what did he confess to Lucy? He wanted 'to be real athletic and have everybody call me "Flash" . . . I'd like to be so good at everything that all around school I'd be known as "Flash".' Charlie is not the only child who has dreamed that dream. In a study by James S. Coleman of the ten representative high schools in northern Illinois, he asked the students to indicate the values that were of greatest importance to them. For girls, beauty outranked every other factor. For boys, athletic ability came in first place (which is just another dimension of physical factors; in other words, size, strength, coordination, and speed can't be separated from physical features themselves). As might be expected, educational achievement ranked very low on both boys' and girls' hierarchy of values.

Because of the status athletes have in today's high schools, I believe this avenue of compensation should be explored by the parents of 'high risk' boys, particularly. If a child is reasonably coordinated he can be taught to play basketball, football, tennis, track, or golf. I have seen some of the most homely adolescents who were highly respected for helping

Thomas Jefferson High School win the championship. As stated before, the key to athletic excellence is to give Junior an early start. We do not hesitate to provide piano lessons to our eight-year-olds; why should we not give basketball training at the same age?

This raises a point of controversy. Many parents feel they do not have the right to force a choice of this nature on their child. They sit back in the hopes that he will make it for himself. However, most children are remarkably unself-disciplined. It is always difficult to learn a new skill – particularly during the initial stages. There is no fun to be derived from total failure, which is the typical feeling in the beginning. Thus, the child never learns those important skills which he will need so badly later on. I recommend that you, his parent, make a careful assessment of his areas of strength. Then select a skill where you believe the greatest possibilities for success lie. Once this selection is made, see to it that he gets through the first stage. Reward him, push him, threaten him, beg him – bribe him if necessary, but make him learn it. If you discover later that you've made a mistake, back up and start over on something else. But don't let inertia keep you from teaching something emotionally useful to your offspring! Does this form of coercion impinge upon the freedom of the child to choose for himself? Perhaps, but so does making him eat properly, keep himself clean, and go to bed at a reasonable hour. It is, as they say, in the child's best interest.

My own dad decided when I was eight years old that he was going to teach me to play tennis. I was not at all enthusiastic about this offer, because it meant hard work. My dad didn't mess around when he decided to teach me something. I knew it meant drill and sweat and blisters. I would much rather have been playing cowboys and Indians with my friends in the neighbourhood. But my dad wanted me to play tennis, and I respected him too much to turn him down. So we spent several agonising Saturdays on the court. He would hit me a ball and I'd whack it over the fence, and then have to go get it. I couldn't have been less motivated, but I tried to act involved. 'You think I'm getting it, Dad?' I said, as another ball flew straight up.

About a month later, however, things began to click. I started to feel good when I hit the ball right. One afternoon, a little fellow my age came up and asked if I'd play him a game. Well, I'd never thought about it, but I didn't see why not. So we played a set of tennis – and I beat him – and I liked that! I slowly began to realise what this game had to offer me. The spark of enthusiasm turned into a flame that still burns. All through high school and college it was my source of self-confidence. If asked to write, 'Who am I?' during the trials of adolescence, I would have begun, 'I am the number-one tennis player in the high school.' If my dad had not planted his thumb in my back, urging me to try something new, I'd have never known what I missed. I am thankful that he helped me compensate. Have you done as much for your child? *Succinctly stated, compensation is your child's best weapon against inferiority.*

Questions and Answers

(1) *My fifteen-year-old is a nature-lover through and through. His room is filled with caged snakes, wasp nests, plants, and insects. Even the garage is occupied by various animals he has caught and tamed. I hate all this stinky stuff and want him to get interested in something else. What should I do?*

If he keeps his zoo clean and well managed, then you should let him follow his interests. Just remember that at fifteen, 'bugs' beat 'drugs' as a hobby!

(2) *My son is an outstanding gymnast. His high-school coach says he has more natural ability than anyone he's ever seen. Yet when he is being judged in a competitive meet, he does terribly! Why does he fail during the most important moments?*

If your son thinks of himself as a failure, his performance will probably match his low self-image when the chips are down. In the same way, there are many excellent golfers in the PGA tour who make a satisfactory living in tournament play, but they never win. They consistently come second, third, sixth, or tenth. Whenever it looks like they might come in first, they 'choke' at the last minute and let someone else win. It is not that they want to fail; rather, they don't 'see' themselves as winners and their performance merely reflects this image.

I talked recently with a concert pianist of outstanding talent who has resolved never to play in public again. She knows she is blessed with remarkable talent, but believes she is a loser in every other regard. Consequently, when she plays the piano on stage, her mistakes and errors make her sound like a beginner. Each time this mortifying experience has occurred, she has become more convinced of her own unworthiness in *every* area. She has now withdrawn into the secluded, quiet, talentless world of the have-nots.

There is no question about it: a lack of self-confidence can completely immobilise a talented person, simply through the threat of failure.

(3) *Is this true of mental ability too? My twelve-year-old was asked to recite a poem at a school function the other day, and he went completely blank in front of the crowd. I know he knew the poem perfectly because he said it dozens of times at home. He's a bright child, but he's had this trouble before. Why does his mind 'turn off' when he's under pressure?*

It will be helpful to understand an important characteristic of intellectual functioning. Your son's self-confidence, or the lack of it, actually affects the way his brain operates. All of us have experienced the frustration of mental 'blocking', which you described. This occurs when a name or fact or idea just won't surface to the conscious mind, even though we *know* it is recorded in the memory. Or suppose we are about to speak to an antagonistic group and our mind suddenly goes blank. This kind of blocking usually occurs (1) when social pressure is great, and (2) when self-confidence is low. Why? *Because emotions affect the efficiency of the human brain.* Unlike a computer, our mental apparatus only functions properly when a delicate biochemical balance exists between the neural cells. This substance makes it possible for a cell to 'fire' its electrochemical charge across the gap (synapse) to another cell. It is now known that a sudden emotional reaction can instantly change the nature of that bio-chemistry, blocking the impulse. This blockage prevents the electrical charge from being relayed and the thought is never generated. This mechanism has profound implications for human behaviour; for example, a child who feels inferior and intellectually inadequate often does not even make use of the mental power with which he has been endowed. His lack of confidence produces a disrupting mental interference, and the two go around and around in an endless cycle of defeat. This is obviously what happened to your son when he 'forgot' the poem.

(4) *What can I do to help him?*

Actually, it is not unusual for a twelve-year-old to 'choke' in front of a crowd. I once stood before three hundred fellow teenagers with my words stuck in my throat and my mind totally out to lunch. It was a painful experience, but time gradually erased its impact. As your child matures, he will probably overcome the problem, if he can experience a few successes to build his confidence. Anything that raises self-esteem will reduce the frequency of mental blocking for children and adults alike.

Strategy No. 5

HELP YOUR CHILD TO COMPETE

A parent who strongly opposes the unfortunate stress currently placed on beauty and brains, as I do, must resolve a difficult philosophical question with regard to his own children. While he recognises the injustice of this value system, he knows his child is forced to compete in a world which worships those attributes. What should he do, then? Should he help his youngster become as attractive as possible? Should he encourage his 'average' child to excel in school? Or would he be wise to de-emphasise these values at home, hoping the child will learn to live with his handicaps?

There are no 'scientific' answers to those questions. I can only give you my considered opinion, in reply. Despite the injustice of this system, my child will not be the one to change it. I am obligated to help him compete in his world as best he can. If his ears protrude, I will have them flattened. If his teeth are crooked, I will see that they are straightened. If he flounders academically, I will seek tutorial assistance to pull him out. He and I are allies in his fight for survival, and I will not turn a deaf ear to his needs.

Rick Barry, the great professional basketball star, is a handsome 6'7'' specimen of health and confidence. Yet as a child he was humiliated and self-conscious about his teeth, even causing him to talk with his hand over his mouth. As he described in the book, *Confessions of a Basketball Gypsy*:

> When my second teeth came in, they came in crooked and two of them were missing in front. Maybe my folks could not afford to have them fixed, or maybe having teeth fixed was not then what it is now. I remember talking to Dad about putting in false teeth in front and wearing braces, which might cut my gums when I exerted myself playing ball. Anyway, I did not have my teeth fixed until I was in college. I was very sensitive about my teeth. I was ashamed to look at myself in the mirror. I used to keep my mouth shut and I'd never smile. I used to keep my hand over my mouth, which muffled my voice and made it hard for people to understand me. I developed this habit of keeping my hand over my mouth, just sort of always resting on my chin, and I couldn't shake it for years afterward.

What similar discomfort is your child experiencing in silence, today? Isn't it our obligation, within the limits of financial resources, to eradicate the flaws which generate the greatest sensitivity? I believe it is, and the job should be done early. Dr. Edward Podolsky, assistant supervisory psychiatrist, Kings County Hospital, New York City, believes physical deformities should be corrected before the child enters the first grade. After that time, his peers will begin to do their 'thing' to his personal esteem.

But we parents must walk a tightrope at this point. While I am helping my child to compete in the world as it is, I must also teach him that its values are temporal and unworthy. Explaining the two contradictory sides of that coin requires considerable skill and tact. How can I urge my daughter to fix her hair neatly and then tell her, 'Beauty doesn't matter'? The key is to begin very early to instruct the child on the *true* values of life: love for all mankind, kindness, integrity, trustworthiness, truthfulness, devotion to God, etc. Physical attractiveness is then described as part of a social game we must play. Since the world is our ball park, we cannot completely ignore the rules of the game. But whether we hit a home run or strike out, we can take comfort in knowing that baseball, itself, is not *that* important. Herein lies an anchor that can hold a child steady.

Questions and Answers

(1) *My thirteen-year-old daughter is still built like a boy, but she is insisting that her mother buy her a bra. Believe me, she has no need for it, and the only reason she wants to wear one is because most of her friends do. Should I give in?*

Your straight and narrow daughter needs a bra to be like her friends, to compete, to avoid ridicule, and to feel like a woman. Those are excellent reasons. Your wife should meet this request by tomorrow morning, if not sooner.

(2) *My older child is a great student and earns straight As year after year. Her younger sister, now in the sixth grade, is completely bored in school and won't even try. The frustrating thing is*

that the younger girl is probably brighter than her older sister.
Why would she refuse to apply her ability like this?

There could be many reasons for her academic disinterest,
but let me suggest the most probable explanation. Children
will often refuse to compete when they think they are likely to
come second instead of first. Therefore, a younger child may
diligently avoid challenging an older sibling in his area of
greatest strength. If Son Number One is a great athlete, then
Son Number Two may be more interested in collecting
butterflies. If Daughter Number One is a disciplined pianist,
then Daughter Number Two may be a boy-crazy goof-off.

This rule does not always hold, of course, depending on
the child's fear of failure and the way he estimates his
chances of successful competition. If his confidence is high,
he may blatantly wade into the territory owned by big
brother, determined to do even better. However, the more
typical response is to seek new areas of compensation which
are not yet dominated by a family superstar.

If this explanation fits the behaviour of your younger
daughter, then it would be wise to accept something less than
perfection from her school performance. Every child need
not fit the same mould – nor can we force them to do so.

(3) *What happens when a child is so different from the group
that he* cannot *compete, no matter how hard he tries?*

That dead-end street is most often responsible for
attempts at self-destruction. I am reminded of a sad little girl
named Lily, an eighth-grader who was referred to me for
psychological counselling. She opened the door to my office
and stood with eyes cast down. Underneath several layers of
powder and makeup, her face was completely aglow with
infected acne. Lily had done her best to bury the inflam-
mation, but she had not been successful. She weighed about
eighty-five pounds and was a physical wreck from head to
toe. She sat down without raising her eyes to mine, lacking
the confidence to face me. I didn't need to ask what was

troubling her. Life had dealt her a devastating blow, and she was bitter, angry, broken, and deeply hurt. The teenager who reaches this point of despair can see no tomorrow. He has no hope. He can't think of anything else. He knows he is repulsive and disgusting. He would like to crawl in a hole, but there is no place to hide. Running away won't help, nor will crying change anything. Too often he chooses suicide as the only way out.

Lily gave me little time to work. The following morning she staggered into the school office and announced that she had swallowed everything in the family medicine cabinet. We laboured feverishly to retrieve the medication and finally succeeded on the way to the hospital. Lily survived physically, but her self-esteem and confidence had died years earlier. The scars on her sad face symbolised the wounds on her adolescent heart.

The incidence of suicide is increasing rapidly among American teenagers. Recent statistics show the number of suicides in some cities has doubled annually for the last few years. Among students nineteen and younger, suicide is now believed to be the third most common cause of death. Studies of these unfortunate children show that they tend to be friendless loners who have been rejected and isolated by their peers. In other words, they have found it impossible to compete successfully in our highly competitive adolescent society. The following statement was taken from the *Los Angeles Times*, May 25, 1971, quoting Dr. Paul Popenoe and others:

Lack of friendship, lack of feelings of acceptance, [and] lack of wholesome social life represent serious problems for high school and college students at all levels. Some studies have shown that 50 per cent of the entire student body has no meaningful social life either inside or outside of school.

Usually, of course, this results in lack of enjoyment of their school life and such students tend to dislike the college they attend. Not merely may their future be permanently handicapped, but more and more the outcome is suicide – now the most common cause of death on a university campus with the exception of automobile accidents, and competent opinion holds that at least half of these accidents are actually suicide. Reported the National Institute of Mental Health, 'Of all the attributes associated with suicidal behaviour, human isolation and withdrawal appears to distinguish those who kill themselves from those who will not.'

A scientist who studies the suicide deaths of school-children in New Jersey found that 'in every case of suicide, the child had no close friends with whom he might share confidences or from whom he received psychological support.'

Obviously, the inability to gain social acceptance is not merely an uncomfortable feeling among the young; such lack of self-esteem can actually extinguish the desire to go on living. Parents and teachers must be taught to recognise the early symptoms of personal despair during the tender, pliable years of childhood, and more importantly, what they can do about it.

Strategy No. 6

DISCIPLINE WITHOUT DAMAGING SELF-ESTEEM

We must deal now with the very important question of discipline and self-esteem. Does punishment, and par-ticularly spanking, break the spirit of the child? The answer to this question depends entirely on the manner and intent of the parents. The issue is not, 'to spank or not to spank'; it is 'how, in what way, and for what?' While this subject was discussed in my book, *Dare to Discipline*, it needs to be re-examined here specifically in relation to the child's self-concept.

A spanking is a very worthwhile tool when used properly, and I strongly urge its periodic application to the bottoms of America's youngest generation. However, like any tool, it can be applied correctly or incorrectly. Belief in corporal punishment is certainly no excuse for taking out your frustrations and anxieties on little Johnny; it won't justify your cracking him behind the ear for his mistakes, accidents, and childish irresponsibility; it offers no licence to punish him in front of others or treat him with general disrespect. I counselled one unfortunate teenager whose brutal father had beaten her throughout childhood. On one occasion after she had accidentally wet her bed during the night, he wrapped her head in the urine-soaked sheet and pushed her into the toilet, upside down. Her self-concept will never recover from the nightmares he inflicted on her tender mind. No one can doubt that this kind of fierce, hostile, undeserved, and whimsical punishment can be devastating to a youngster, particularly when he knows he isn't loved at home. There are, then, many psychological dangers to be avoided in this area.

On the other hand, another highly effective way to damage self-esteem is to go to the opposite extreme – avoiding disciplinary control altogether. When a child knows he has done wrong, being selfish or offensive to others, he expects his parents to respond appropriately. After all, they are the symbols of justice, law, and order which every child loves. Their refusal to accept his challenge is viewed with disrespect, making them unworthy of his allegiance. But more importantly, he wonders why they would let him do such harmful things if they really love him. In the Book of Hebrews, chapter 12, verse 8 (REVISED STANDARD VERSION) this bit of wisdom is stated explicitly:

If you are left without discipline, in which all have participated, then you are illegitimate children and not sons.

How true this is! An undisciplined child feels like he does not belong in the family, despite the 'love' of his parents. This bit of biblical wisdom was confirmed by Stanley Coopersmith, associate professor of psychology, University of

California. Dr. Coopersmith studied 1,738 normal middle-class boys and their families, beginning in the preadolescent period and following them through to young manhood. After identifying those boys having the highest self-esteem, he compared their homes and childhood influences with those having a lower sense of self-worth. He found three important characteristics which distinguished them: (1) The high-esteem children were clearly more loved and appreciated at home than were the low-esteem boys. The parental love was deep and genuine, not just an empty display of words. The boys knew they were the object of pride and interest, increasing their own sense of self-worth. (2) The high-esteem group came from homes where parents had been significantly more strict in their approach to discipline. By contrast, the parents of the low-esteem group had created insecurity and dependence by their permissiveness. Their children were more likely to feel that the rules were not enforced because no one cared enough to get involved. ('If you are left without discipline – then you are illegitimate children and not sons.') Furthermore, the most successful and independent young men during the latter period of the study were found to have come from homes that demanded the strictest accountability and responsibility. And as could have been predicted, the family ties remained the strongest – not in the wishy-washy homes – but in the homes where discipline and self-control had been a way of life. (3) The homes of the high-esteem group were also characterised by democracy and openness. Once the boundaries for behaviour were established, there was freedom for individual personalities to grow and develop. The boys could express themselves without fear of ridicule, and the overall atmosphere was marked by acceptance and emotional safety.

Dr. Joseph Bobbitt, the well-known child psychologist, expressed this same concept as follows: 'There have been studies showing that the child who has the lowest self-esteem is the one who isn't permitted to say anything at the dinner table. The one with the next lowest image of himself is the child who is allowed to dominate conversation. Highest on the list is the youngster whose parents tell him, "Yes, you can speak up – when it's your turn." ' That statement reveals the important balance between love and control which produces emotionally secure and healthy children.

If good discipline is so important to the building of self-esteem, then, let's discuss its ingredients. Returning to the subject of spanking, when and under what circumstances is it appropriate to use this form of discipline? You will not damage your child emotionally if you follow this philosophy: (1) Establish the boundaries in advance. Tell the child before he breaks the rule just what the rule is. Make sure he knows what you expect, and why. There should be no ex post facto guilt! (2) When he defiantly challenges your authority by disobeying your instructions, then he will expect you to act. Don't disappoint him. A spanking, therefore, is to be reserved for that moment of conflict when the child dares you to defend your right to lead. It should come in response to his sassiness, haughtiness, or outright disobedience. NO OTHER FORM OF DISCIPLINE IS AS EFFECTIVE AS A SPANKING WHEN WILFUL DEFIANCE IS INVOLVED. In this sense, corporal punishment is not a 'last resort' to be applied after you have screamed, yelled, cried, begged, deprived, wept, and stood him in the corner. It is to be used any time he chooses to stiffen his neck, clench his fists, and toss his little toe across the line you've drawn in the dirt. (3) Do not spank the child for mistakes and accidents. Do not spank him for forgetting to feed the dog, or make his bed, or other acts of immaturity. Do not spank him to help him learn his lessons. (Flip Wilson said, 'Spanking a child to help him learn something I cannot defend. How can you 'speck him to learn anything when you're whacking upon his rear end?' I agree.) Do not spank him for something today which was ignored yesterday. This kind of behaviour does not represent wilful defiance on the part of the child, and he will resent being punished for triggering your wrath accidentally. (4) After the spanking, Johnny will probably want to be loved and reassured. By all means, open your arms and let him come! Hold him close and tell him of your love. Rock him gently and let him know, again, why he was punished and how he can avoid the trouble next time. You cannot talk to a child in this heart-to-heart fashion while you are still in conflict; understanding and closeness are not achieved by sending an angry, defiant child to his room to pout. This moment of communication is created by the emotional ventilation brought on by an appropriate spanking, and it does not destroy self-esteem. It builds love, fidelity, and family unity. (5) Your spankings should be completed by the time a child is eight or nine years old. Never spank a teenager! Since the self-esteem of an adolescent is in serious doubt anyway, a spanking is the ultimate insult, making him feel like a baby.

There are many specialists in child development today who recommend trying to 'reason' the child out of his defiance. Anyone who has ever tried to do that knows it is impossible. Why? Because the issue of 'who's toughest?' is very important to children. Whenever a child moves to a new neighbourhood, he often has to fight (verbally or physically) to establish himself on the hierarchy of strength. A teacher will certainly have to defend himself in the first few days of the school year, because the entire class wants to know if he's strong or weak. Regardless of what the parent and child are fighting over, the *real* issue is this: are you in charge or am I? And when the stage is set for that battle, reason and explanation simply will not settle the matter.

Those same specialists also say that a spanking teaches your child to hit others, making him a more violent person. Nonsense! If your child has ever bumped his arm against a hot stove, you can bet he'll never deliberately do that again. He does not become a more violent person because the stove burnt him; in fact, he learned a valuable lesson from the pain. Similarly, when he falls out of his high chair or smashes his finger in the door or is bitten by a grumpy dog, he learns about physical dangers in his world. These bumps and bruises throughout childhood are nature's way of teaching him what to fear. They do not damage his self-esteem. They do not make him vicious. They merely acquaint him with reality. In like manner, an appropriate spanking from a loving parent provides the same service. It tells him there are not only physical dangers to be avoided, but he must steer clear of some social traps as well (selfishness, defiance, dishonesty, unprovoked aggression, etc.).

Finally, I must refer back to the original question: does punishment, particularly spanking, break the spirit of the child? It is very important to understand the difference between breaking the *spirit* of the child, and breaking his *will*. The human spirit is exceedingly fragile at all ages and must be handled with care. It involves a person's view of himself, his personal worth, and the emotional factors to which this book is dedicated. A parent can damage his child's spirit very easily — by ridicule, disrespect, threats to withdraw love, and by verbal rejection. Anything that depreciates his self-esteem is costly to his spirit. However, while the spirit is brittle and must be treated gently, the will is made of steel. It is full strength at the moment of birth, as any midnight bottle-warmer knows. Even a child whose spirit has been crushed can present the most awesome display of wilful power. *We want, then, to shape the will of a child, but leave his spirit intact.* This is done by requiring reasonable obedience to predetermined commands, and then winning the battles he chooses to initiate. If you permit your youngster's will to remain unbridled, the result is often extreme self-will, which makes him useless, to himself, others, or even to God.

Questions and Answers

(1) *Why is there so much confusion on the subject of discipline today? Is it really that difficult to raise our children properly?*

Parents are confused because they have been taught an illogical, unworkable approach to child management, by many professionals who ought to know better. The authorities on the subject of discipline had muddied the water with permissive philosophies which contradict the very nature of children. Let me cite an example. *Growing*

Pains is a question-and-answer book for parents, published by the American Academy of Pediatrics (a division of the American Medical Association). The following question written by a parent is quoted in the book, along with the answer provided below.

CHILD SLAMS DOOR IN PARENT'S FACE

Q. What does one do when an angry child slams a door in one's face?

A. Step back. Then do nothing until you have reason to believe that the child's anger has cooled off. Trying to reason with an angry person is like hitting your head against a stone wall.

When the child is in a good mood, explain to him how dangerous door-slamming can be. Go so far as to give him a description of how a person can lose a finger from a slammed door. Several talks of this sort are generally enough to cure a door-slammer.

How inadequate is this reply, from my point of view. The writer failed to recognise that the door-slamming behaviour was *not* the real issue in this situation. To the contrary, the child was demonstrating his defiance of parental authority, and for *that* he should have been held accountable. Instead, the parent is told to wait until the child is in a good mood (which could be next Thursday), and then talk about the dangers of door-slamming. It seems clear that the child was begging his mom to accept his challenge, but she was in the other room counting to ten and keeping cool. And let's all wish her lots of luck on the next encounter.

As I've stated, the great givers of parental advice have failed to offer a course of action to be applied in response to a wilful defiance. In the situation described above, for example, what is Mom supposed to do until Junior cools off? What if he is breaking furniture and writing on the back of that slammed door? What if he calls her dirty names and whacks his little sister across the mouth? You see, the *only* tool given to Mom by the writer, above, is postponed *reason*. And as every mother knows, reason is practically worthless in response to anger and disrespect.

Nature has provided a wonderfully padded place for use in moments of haughty defiance, and I wish the disciplinary 'experts' were less confused as to its proper purpose.

Q. *Is it true that the 'middle child' has greater problems with low self-esteem than other members of the family? Maybe that explains why my second son has never been a confident person.*

Low self-esteem can become a problem for any human being, regardless of birth order or age. However, you are right in assuming that the middle child sometimes finds it more difficult to establish his identity within the family. He enjoys neither the status of the eldest nor the attention given to the baby. Furthermore, he is likely to be born at a busy period in the life of his parents, and especially his mother. Then when he reaches the toddler years, his precious territory is invaded by a cute little newborn who steals Mama from him. Is it any wonder that he often asks, 'Who am I and where is my place in life?'

I would recommend that parents take steps to ensure the identity of *all* their children, but especially the child in the middle. That can be accomplished by occasionally relating to each boy or girl as individuals, rather than merely as members of the group. Let me offer two suggestions that may serve as examples that well illustrate what I mean.

(1) Ask each offspring to design his own flag, which can then be sewn in canvas or cloth. That flag is then flown in the front yard on the child's 'special' days, including birthdays, after he has received an *A* in school, when he scores a goal in soccer, or hits a home run in baseball, and so forth.

(2) It is meaningful for Dad to 'date' each child, *one at a time*, every four or five weeks. The other kids should not be told where they are going, until it is revealed

by the boy or girl in retrospect. They can play miniature golf, go bowling, play basketball, eat tacos or pizza, or visit a skating rink. The choice should be made by the child whose turn has arrived.

There are other ways to accomplish the same purpose. The target, again, is to plan activities that emphasise one child's individuality apart from his identity within the group.

Q. The children in our neighbourhood are so brutal to each other. They ridicule and name-call and fight from morning to night. Is there anything that we, as parents, can do about this?

Parents in a neighbourhood can bring about a more peaceful atmosphere among their children, *if* they will talk to each other, but that takes some doing! There is no quicker way to anger one mother than for another woman to criticise her precious cub. It is a delicate subject, indeed. Thus, the typical neighbourhood provides little 'feedback' to parents in regard to the behaviour of their children. The children know there are no lines of communication between adults and they take advantage of the barrier. What each block needs is a mother who has the courage to say, 'I want to be told what my child does when he is beyond his own yard. If he is a brat with other children, I would like to know it. If he is disrespectful with adults, please mention it to me. I will not consider it tattling and I won't resent your coming to me. I hope I can share my insights regarding your children, too. None of our children is perfect, and we'll know better how to teach them if we can talk openly to each other as adults.'

In summary, children are capable of learning social skills very early in life, and it is our task to make them 'feel' for others.

(3) My little girl is sometimes sugar-sweet, and other times she is unbearably irritating. How can I get her out of a bad mood when she has not really done anything to deserve punishment?

I would suggest that you take her in your arms and talk to her in this manner: 'I don't know whether you've noticed it or not, but you have two "personalities". A personality is a way of acting and talking and behaving. One of your personalities is sweet and loving. No one could possibly be more lovable and happy when this personality is in control. It likes to work and look for ways to make the rest of the family happy. And all you have to do is press a little red button, "ding", to call it out.

'But then sometimes you push another button, "ding", and out comes the other personality. It is cranky and noisy and silly. It wants to fight with your brother and disobey your mom. It gets up grouchy in the morning and complains throughout the day.

'Now, I know that you can press the button for the neat personality or you can call up the mean one. Sometimes it takes a swat or two to make you press the right button. If you keep on pressing the wrong button, like you have been today, then I'm going to make you uncomfortable, one way or the other. I'm tired of that cranky character and I want to see the grinny one. Can we make a deal?'

When discipline becomes a game, as in a conversation such as this, then you've achieved your purpose without conflict and animosity.

Strategy No. 7

KEEP A CLOSE EYE ON THE CLASSROOM

What should a parent do when he knows his child is not achieving in school? First, he must understand that academic failure is a symptom of a more specific cause. There is a great difference, for example, between the under-achiever who refuses to work and the slow learner who is *unable* to do what is required. Before we can help the child, therefore, we must diagnose his problem. Most school districts now have school psychologists who will administer a battery of diagnostic tests when needed for a particular child. Concerned parents can initiate this action by calling the guidance office and requesting that an assessment be made. If the local school district does not offer this free service, it might be necessary to seek assistance from a psychologist in private practice.

Once the nature of the difficulty is known, steps can be taken to resolve it. Listed below are some suggestions which might be helpful:

(1) Tutorial assistance can pull a child through a rough spot, academically. Particularly in reference to the three Rs, some children have trouble grasping the concepts while sitting in a classroom. There are too many distractions and too few reasons to concentrate. However, when a tutor can work with a child on a one-to-one basis, learning is much more likely to occur. The school is your best resource in finding a patient, skilled tutor.

(2) Make certain your child has learned to read by the end of his second year in school. I'm convinced that self-esteem has more frequently been assassinated over reading problems than any other aspect of school life. And it is all so unnecessary! Educators have developed many creative approaches to remedial reading – involving teaching machines, more simplified alphabets, multisensory instruction, and other techniques. Every child, with *very* few exceptions, can learn to read if taught properly. Unfortunately, however, these techniques are often expensive and may not be provided in your child's classroom. The typical group-teaching approach may be the only programme offered, with its high failure rate. Here again, tutorial assistance is strongly recommended in these cases. *It is absolutely critical to your child's self-concept that he learn to read early in his school career, and if the professional educators can't do the job, someone else will!*

(3) If you have a confirmed, hardcore 'underachiever' – a child who absolutely refuses to use the ability he

has – you have been blessed with a most frustrating academic problem. I'm sure you already knew that. All of the screaming, yelling, punishing, crying, and depriving produce little more than a yawn and another *F*. I have tried many approaches to motivate these happy-go-lucky playboys and found most of them to be unsuccessful. The one alternative which has been workable has involved a carefully conceived plan of immediate rewards. It is not sufficient, however, to merely bribe a child for working; that produces a short-term fizzle of energy, followed by further apathy and more yawns. In my book *Dare to Discipline* I have discussed the principles of reward and reinforcement in considerable detail, specifically as applied to the underachiever. The parent of a child with such a problem may wish to consult that reference.

(4) What will we do for the self-esteem of the slow learner? The question demands an answer because there are so many children in this fix. Intelligence quotients in the total population are distributed around a midpoint of 100. This means, in essence, that 50 per cent of the children have IQ's above 100, and 50 per cent score below that point. Now, obviously, those youngsters in the lower half of the school population are in a high-risk category for learning problems and the self-doubts they bring. The farther down the IQ distribution we go, the more likely we are to find children who face failure as a daily routine in the classroom. Approximately 22 per cent of the children in America have IQ's between 70 and 90 – intellectual boundaries marking the slow-learner category. *Before they even enter first grade, it can be predicted that most of these children will soon develop feelings of inadequacy and inferiority.* Thus, we know by the distribution of intelligence that one-fourth to one-half of our children will eventually enter adult life having had twelve years' ex-

perience in feeling dumb. They will never forget it!

I offer two strong recommendations to the parents of a slow learner: First, de-emphasise academic achievement as a value in your home. This may seem like heresy in an educationally oriented, middle-class society. However, I return to my thesis: self-esteem crumbles when the necessary attributes are beyond reach. Anything that your child *cannot* accomplish, despite his best efforts, should be toned down in importance. You would not demand that a crippled child become a track star, yet every parent wants his 'average' student to become a college graduate. If I had a child with an IQ of 85 who was struggling to do what other children accomplished with ease, I would do my best to remove the pressure from his back. I would concentrate on his strengths and say as little as possible about his unimpressive report card. There are some things in life which are more important than success in school, and self-esteem is one of them. If forced to choose between these two features, my child's sense of worth will receive top priority.

Secondly, a parent should not allow the school to 'fail' his slow learner after kindergarten. I can think of few circumstances which justify an incapable child being retained in the same grade twice. This creates an image of failure that is devastating to a child's sense of adequacy. What can he conclude, other than that he is incredibly stupid? All of his friends were promoted to the next grade. Why wasn't he? Now look at him, stuck in the same classroom with all the babies! What self-hatred this archaic educational practice has wrought in the lives of its victims. And unfortunately, retention for the slow learner accomplishes nothing academically. He does not get brighter next year, nor do his basic skills suddenly bubble forth. The only thing that changes the second time around is his self-concept, which then has a sizeable crack running from top to bottom.

The slow learner needs parental help in finding his compensating skills, coupled with the assurance that his personal worth does not depend on success in academia.

(5) There are times when a change of schools – or even a change of teachers within a school – can be in the child's best interest. Educators are reluctant to approve these transfers, for obvious reasons, although the possibility should be considered when the situation demands it. Schools vary tremendously in their difficulty; some are located in higher socio-economic areas where a majority of the children are much more intelligent than would ordinarily be expected. The mean IQ in schools of this nature may fall between 115–120. What happens, then, to a child with average ability in such a setting? Although he might have competed successfully in an ordinary school, he is in the lower fifteen per cent at Einstein Elementary. My point is this: success is not absolute, it is relative. A child does not ask, 'How am I doing?' but rather, 'How am I doing compared to everyone else?' Little Johnny may grow up thinking he is a dummy when he would have been an intellectual leader in a less competitive setting. Thus, if a child is floundering in one academic environment, the solution might involve a transfer to a more suitable classroom.

In conclusion, the topic of 'learning problems' is much too comprehensive to be covered adequately in this brief section. However, the theme running through these comments is an important one: parents should be informed regarding the educational progress of their children, intervening appropriately when necessary. Their purpose should be to maximise educational potential without sacrificing self-esteem.

Questions and Answers

(1) *Do slow learners and mentally handicapped children have the same needs for esteem that others have?*

Sometimes I wish they didn't, but their needs are no different. During a portion of my training at Pacific State Hospital for the Mentally Retarded, Pomona, California, I was impressed by the vast need for love shown by some of the most retarded patients. There were times when I would step into the door of a children's ward and forty or more severely retarded youngsters would rush towards me screaming, 'Daddy! Daddy! Daddy!' They would push and shove around my legs with their arms extended upward, making it difficult to avoid falling. Their deep longings to be loved simply couldn't be satisfied in the group experiences of hospital life, despite the exceptionally high quality of Pacific State.

The need for esteem has led me to favour a current trend in education, whereby the borderline mentally retarded children are given special assistance in their regular classrooms without segregating them in special classes. The stigma of being a 'retard', as they call themselves, is no less insulting for a ten-year-old that it would be for you or me.

(2) *What do you think of the 'new math', which has been adopted in American schools?*

The 'new math', which is no longer very new, represents a noble attempt to teach mathematical concepts to children, rather than mechanical rote processes. In other words, the purpose is to help children understand the meaning of math instead of memorising how to divide, borrow, count decimal places, and so on. I have found that this new approach is great for children who have the conceptual power to grasp the principles being taught. Unfortunately, about half the schoolchildren do not possess the higher mental ability needed to handle this kind of abstract reasoning. My concern is with that confused 50 per cent: what are we doing for them? At least with the 'old math' they learned how to handle basic arithmetical computations, even if they didn't understand them all.

In brief, I would favour a continuation of the present effort to challenge our brighter students, but we must provide a more concrete programme for the blank-eyed little fellows who just don't get the message.

(3) *What part does intelligence play in the self-esteem of adults? Do they tend to forget the trouble they had during the school years?*

It has been said that 'a boy is the father of the man', meaning we grown-ups are direct products of our own childhood. Thus, everything I have said about self-esteem in children applies to adults as well. We are all graduates of the educational 'fail factory', and few have escaped completely unscathed. Furthermore, our self-worth is *still* being evaluated on the basis of intelligence. Dr. Richard Herrnstein, a Harvard University psychologist, predicts that a caste system founded on IQ is coming to America. He believes people will soon be locked into rigid intellectual classes which will determine careers, earning power, and social status. Dr. Herrnstein's expectation is based on the disintegration of racial and sexual barriers to success, leaving only intelligence as the major remaining discrimination in America. I don't agree fully with Dr. Herrnstein, although I am certain we will see the continuing importance of mental ability to self-esteem in our technological world.

Strategy No. 8
Avoid Overprotection and Dependency

Now let's look at the threats to self-esteem that must come as your child matures. From about three years of age, your little pride and joy begins making his way into the world of other people. He plays near his home with neighbourhood children; he is often enrolled in nursery school, and a year or two later, he will toddle off to kindergarten. Whereas his self-concept could be carefully guarded during the first few years, it now becomes very difficult for Mom to control his environment. Other children may mock him and laugh at his deficiencies; he may be incapable of competing in their games; or he might even be crippled or killed in an accident of some kind. This initial 'turning loose' period is often extremely threatening to his compulsive mother. Her natural reaction is to hold her baby close to her breast, smothering him in 'protection'. By watching, guarding, defending, and shielding him night and day, perhaps she can spare him some of the pain she experienced in her own younger days. However, her intense desire to help may actually interfere with his growth and development. Certain risks must be tolerated if a child is to learn and progress; he will never learn to walk if he is not allowed to fall down in the process.

It is probably easier to foster an unhealthy dependency relationship between parent and child than it is to avoid one. It often begins during the early days of infancy. At the moment of birth, a little child is completely and totally helpless. One forgets just how dependent a newborn is – in fact, I want to forget it, just as soon as possible! That little creature lying there can do nothing for himself: he doesn't roll over, he can't scratch his head, he is unable to verbalise his thoughts, and he won't lift a finger in his own behalf. Consequently, his parents are responsible for meeting his every need. They are his servants, and if they're too slow in meeting his demands, he is equipped with a spine-chilling scream to urge them into action. He bears no obligations whatsoever. He doesn't even have to appreciate their efforts. He won't say 'please' or 'thank you'; he doesn't apologise for getting them up six times in one night; he even offers no sympathy when at 3.01 a.m. his exhausted mom drives the point of a safety pin through the fleshy part of her thumb (without doubt, the greatest agony in human experience!).

In other words, a child begins his life in a state of complete and total dependency on those whose name he bears.

About twenty years later, however, at the other end of childhood, we expect some radical changes to have occurred in that individual. He should then be able to assume the full responsibilities of young adulthood. He is expected to spend his money wisely, hold down a job, be loyal to one woman, support the needs of his family, obey the laws of the land, and be a good citizen. In other words, during the course of childhood, an individual should progress from a position of *no* responsibility to a position of full responsibility. Now, friends and neighbours, how does little John-John get from position A to position B? How does this magical transformation of self-discipline take place? There are many self-appointed experts on child raising who seem to feel it all should happen towards the latter end of adolescence, about fifteen minutes before Big John leaves home permanently. Prior to that time, he should be allowed to do whatever he wishes at the moment.

I reject that notion categorically. The best preparation for responsible adulthood is derived from training in responsibility during childhood. This is not to say that the child is horsewhipped into acting like an adult. It does mean that the child be encouraged to progress on an orderly timetable of events, carrying the level of responsibility that is appropriate for his age. Shortly after birth, for example, the mother begins transferring responsibilities from her shoulders to those of her infant. Little by little he learns to sleep through the night, hold his own bottle, and reach for what he wants. Later he is potty-trained (hopefully), and he learns to walk and talk. Gradually, as each new skill is mastered, his mother 'frees' herself that much more from his servitude.

The transfer of responsibility ordinarily runs along smoothly until the child reaches about eighteen months of age. At that point, he suddenly realises two things: (1) Work is definitely an evil to be avoided at all costs! He hates the very thought of it! (2) With every new task he is forced to accept, he loses his momma a little more. Whereas she was his full-time servant before, now she is slipping away. He must pick up his blocks – she isn't going to do it for him anymore. He must wash behind his ears – she won't be there to wield the washcloth next time. And at this age, he craves adult attention. Therefore, if he is going to retain his playmate, he'd better keep her on the job. His thoughts are not this conscious or rational, of course, but anyone who has ever raised a toddler knows it happens! Consequently, a great tug-of-war ensues. Mom is trying to get Junior to grow up, and he's trying to maintain his infancy.

Enter again the emotional and physical threats of which I've spoken. They can easily cause an anxious mother to turn loose of the rope in the tug-of-war described above. Her idea is: 'If I keep him dependent upon me for as long as possible, I can better protect him from the cruel world.' Therefore, she won't let him cross the street for several years after he could make it safely. She does *everything* for him, requiring nothing in return. She enters into each neighbourhood argument that occurs among his friends, taking his side regardless of who was right. Later she walks him to school, holding his hand with the proud assurance that she is being a good mother. and heaven help the teacher who tries to discipline her little tiger! You see, all through childhood she fosters a continuation of the infancy relationship, retaining all the responsibility on her back.

Does Junior prosper under this setup? Of course not. Mother is giving of herself totally, which seems like a loving thing to do. However, at the same time, she is allowing her overprotected child to fall behind his normal timetable in preparation for ultimate release as a young adult. As a ten-year-old, he can't make himself do anything unpleasant, since he has never had any experience in handling the difficult. He does not know how to 'give' to anyone else, for he has only thought of himself. He finds it hard to make decisions or exercise any kind of self-discipline. A few years later, he will steamroll into adolescence completely unprepared for the freedom and responsibility he will find there. And finally, his future wife is in for some swell surprises which I shudder to contemplate.

Marguerite and Willard Beecher, authors of an excellent book called *Parents on the Run*, first described the concept I have presented. They stated, and I strongly agree, that *the parent must gain his freedom from the child, so that the child can gain his freedom from the parent*. Think about that for a moment. If you never get free from your child by transferring responsibility to him, then he remains hopelessly bound to you, too! You have knotted each other in a paralysing interdependency which stifles growth and development.

I recently counselled a mother whose husband had died when their only son, Davie, was a baby. She had been left with the terrifying task of raising this lad by herself, and Davie was the only person left in the world whom she really loved. Her reaction was to smother him totally. The boy was seven years of age when she came to me. He was afraid to sleep in a room by himself. He refused to stay with a baby-sitter, and he even resisted going to school. He did not dress himself and his behaviour was infantile in every regard. In fact, instead of waiting in the reception room while I talked to his mother, he found my office and stood with his hand on the doorknob for an hour, whimpering and begging to be admitted. His mother interpreted all of this as evidence of his fear that she would die, as his father had done. In response, she bound him even more tightly to her, sacrificing all her own needs and desires: she could neither go on dates nor bring any men into their home; she could not get involved in any activities of her own or have any adult experiences without her cling-along son. You see, she had never gained her freedom from Davie, and in turn, Davie had not gained his freedom from his lovin' momma.

Have you allowed your child to enjoy the freedom and responsibility that are appropriate for his age? Does your fear of emotional and physical hardships keep him locked in your arms? Are you afraid to make him work because he protests so loudly? I have discovered that this process of dependency may not always be motivated by an admirable desire to protect the child. *Very* often, a mother will foster a binding relationship because she has emotional needs of her own. Perhaps the romance has gone out of her marriage, leaving her child as her only real source of love. Perhaps she has had trouble making lasting friendships. For whatever reason, she wants to be the 'heavy' in the life of her child. (I'm certain Davie's mom had this need.) Thus, she waits on him hand and foot. She refuses to obtain her freedom for the specific purpose of denying him his. I know one mother-daughter team which maintained this interlocutory relationship until the mother's death at ninety-four years of age. The daughter, then seventy-two, found herself unmarried, alone, and on her own for the first time in her life. It's a frightening thing to experience in old age what other people endure in adolescence.

As indicated, this vital task of turning a child loose is not restricted to the early years. It is equally important all the way through his march towards young adulthood. Each year he should make more of his own decisions than in the prior twelve months; the routine responsibilities of living should fall to his shoulders as he is able to handle them. A seven-year-old, for example, is usually capable of selecting his own clothing for the day. He should be keeping his room straight and making his bed each morning. A nine- or ten-year-old may be carrying more freedom, such as in the choice of television programmes to watch (within reason). I am not suggesting that we abdicate parental leadership altogether; rather, I believe we should give conscious thought to the reasonable, orderly transfer of *freedom* and *responsibility*, so that we are preparing the child each year for that moment of full independence which must come. The twenty-year process of 'letting go' is diagrammed on page 121, with examples of independence to be added as he grows.

Now, I have a very important message at this point, of particular relevance to Christian parents. Others are invited to read along, but may not comprehend its full significance. I have observed that the process of 'letting go' during the late adolescence is much more difficult for parents with deep, religious convictions than for those without them. Christian

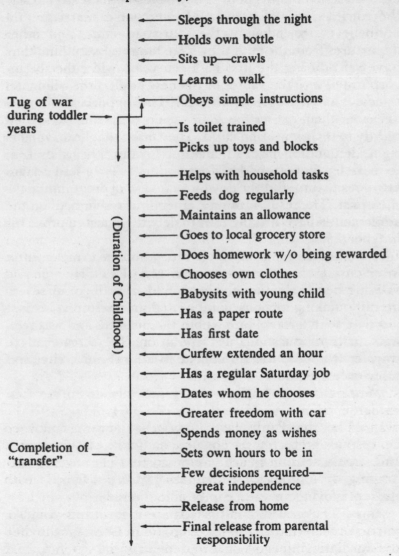

BIRTH

(no responsibility)

Tug of war during toddler years →

(Duration of Childhood)

- Sleeps through the night
- Holds own bottle
- Sits up—crawls
- Learns to walk
- Obeys simple instructions
- Is toilet trained
- Picks up toys and blocks
- Helps with household tasks
- Feeds dog regularly
- Maintains an allowance
- Goes to local grocery store
- Does homework w/o being rewarded
- Chooses own clothes
- Babysits with young child
- Has a paper route
- Has first date
- Curfew extended an hour
- Has a regular Saturday job
- Dates whom he chooses
- Greater freedom with car
- Spends money as wishes
- Sets own hours to be in
- Few decisions required— great independence
- Release from home
- Final release from parental responsibility

Completion of "transfer" →

YOUNG ADULTHOOD

(full responsibility)

families are more likely to be aware of, and be concerned by, the spiritual dangers their children will face with increasing independence and freedom. They have greater reason to fear the consequences of premarital intercourse, marriage to a nonbeliever, rejection of the Christian ethic, and other departures from the faith they have taught. Everything they have said during the first eighteen years will either be incorporated into the values of the new adult, or it will be all rejected and thrown overboard. The importance of this decision, then, causes too many zealous parents to hold on tightly to their maturing child. They insist that he do what is right, demanding his obedience and loyalty. They allow him to make few important decisions and try to force-feed certain attitudes to him. But the day for that kind of programming is then past. The result is often tremendous resentment on the adolescent's part, leading him to defy them just to prove his independence.

A mother with this 'hang-on' attitude came to me recently in regard to her twenty-year-old son, Paul. He was not obeying her as she thought he should, and the conflict was literally making her sick. Paul rented an apartment against her will, with a roommate whom she disliked, and was seen with girls of questionable reputation. He threatened to transfer from a Christian college to a local university, and more or less denounced his faith.

'What can I do? What can I possibly do to get him straightened out?' she asked.

I told her that Paul's day-to-day behaviour was no longer her responsibility. She had completed her task as his mother and should set him free. I explained that her nagging and begging were probably accentuating Paul's defiance, since she was playing an inappropriate 'mothering' role which he resented. I suggested that this woman sit down and write her son a polite and loving letter, telling him emphatically that she was letting him go – once and for all.

Several days later, the woman brought a rough draft of a letter she had written for my approval – but it was not what I had in mind. Her composition turned out to be a finger-wagging indictment, warning of the future and urging the wayward boy back to his senses. It was impossible to edit what she had written – so I wrote a letter for her. She sent my letter to her son over her own signature, and I have printed it below with her permission:

Dear Paul:

This is the most important letter I have ever written to you, and I hope you will take it as seriously as it is intended. I have given a great amount of thought and prayer to the matter I want to convey, and believe I am right in what I've decided to do.

For the past several years, you and I have been involved in a painful tug-of-war. You have been struggling to free yourself of my values and my wishes for your life. At the same time, I have been trying to hold you to what we both know is right. Even at the risk of nagging, I have been saying, 'Go to church,' 'Choose the right friends,' 'Make good grades in school,' 'Live a Christian life,' 'Prepare wisely for your future,' etc. I'm sure you've gotten tired of this urging and warning, but I have only wanted the best for you. This is the only way I knew to keep you from making some of the mistakes so many others have made.

However, I've thought all of this over during the last month and I believe that my job as your mother is now finished. Since the day you were born, I have done my best to do what was right for you. I have not always been successful – I've made mistakes and I've failed in many ways. Someday you will learn how difficult it is to be a good parent, and perhaps then you'll understand me better than you do now. But there's one area where I have never wavered: I've loved you with everything that is within me. It is impossible to convey the depth of my love for you through these years, and that affection is as great today as it's ever been. It will continue to be there in the future, although our relationship will change from this moment. As of now, you are free! You may reject

God or accept Him, as you choose. Ultimately, you will answer only to Him, anyway. You may marry whomever you wish without protest from me. You may go to U.C.L.A. or U.S.C. or any other college of your selection. You may fail or succeed in each of life's responsibilities. The umbilical cord is now broken.

I am not saying these things out of bitterness or anger. I still care what happens to you and am concerned for your welfare. I will pray for you daily, and if you come to me for advice, I'll offer my opinion. *But the responsibility now shifts from my shoulders to yours*. You are a man now, and you're entitled to make your own decisions – regardless of the consequences. Throughout your life I've tried to build a foundation of values which would prepare you for this moment of manhood and independence. That time has come, and my record is in the books.

I have confidence in you, son. You are gifted and have been blessed in so many ways. I believe God will lead you and guide your footsteps, and I am optimistic about the future. Regardless of the outcome, I will always have a special tenderness in my heart for my beloved son.

Sincerely,
Your mother

This message simply must be conveyed to your child when the time comes, whether it be discussed in conversation or written in the form of a letter. We are given eighteen or twenty years to interject the proper values and attitudes; then we must take our hands off and trust in divine leadership to influence the outcome. And surprisingly, the chances of a young adult making the right decisions are greatly increased when he is not having to fight for his manhood and independence.

The biblical story of the Prodigal Son in the Book of Luke is a brilliant guide to follow at this point. The father knew that his boy was going to squander his money and live with prostitutes. He knew he would make many mistakes, and possibly destroy himself in the process. Yet he permitted the young man to leave home! He did not chain him to a tree, or even condemn him verbally. Nor did he bail him out when he ran aground in the distant land. The love with which the father said goodbye made it possible for his son to return after making a mess of his life. We would do well to follow the father's loving example.

In summary, our final task in building self-esteem for our children is in transferring responsibility from our shoulders to theirs, beginning with the rudimentary skills of infancy, and terminating with their emancipation during the late teens or early twenties. Letting go is not an easy task, but good parenthood demands it.

Questions and Answers

(1) *Can you help me better understand the difference between* irresponsible *versus* defiant *behaviour in my children? Why is the distinction important to me as a parent?*

The distinction deals with your child's *intention*, which is all-important in deciding how to respond as a parent. Suppose little Johnny is acting silly at the table and spills his milk. He did not intend to knock over the glass, but it happened. Or perhaps he leaves his bicycle out in the rain, or loses his schoolbooks. These behaviours result from his childish irresponsibility, and should be handled accordingly. It would be wrong to spank a child for being a child, in my view. Rather, these occurrences should offer opportunities to teach him to be more responsible. You may make him work to repair the damage, or temporarily deprive him of the item he has abused. However, I feel strongly that a child should never be spanked for mistakes or behaviour that he didn't know were wrong, unless it involves a matter of extreme danger (running in the street, invading the medicine cabinet, etc.).

By contrast, defiant behaviour is very different from childish irresponsibility. It is headstrong and wilful. It is premeditated and calculating. In short, it is intentional, and deserves immediate disciplinary action.

Perhaps an illustration will help at this point. When my daughter was five years old, she was given a baby hamster for Christmas. Being an incurable animal lover, she became extremely fond of the furry little creature. I noticed at once, however, that she lacked the responsibility to take care of the pet properly. Repeatedly I warned her to keep the door closed on its cage and provide enough food and water for its survival. Despite my intervention, I returned home one day to find my daughter exhausted and red-eyed from crying. Sure enough, she had left the cage door open and our world-famous dachshund, Siggie (Sigmund Freud) had sent the hamster on to its untimely reward. When my daughter found its stiff, bloody little body near its cage, she was broken-hearted.

What, then, was to be my response? I had told her repeatedly how to care for the hamster, but she had failed to do so. Nevertheless, it would have been wrong for me to lash her for this mistake. Instead, I took her in my arms and held her until she stopped crying. Then I talked softly to her in these terms: 'Danae, you know that I told you what would happen if you didn't take care of your hamster. But you were thinking about something else and now he's dead. I'm not mad at you, because you haven't done anything mean. You have just behaved like a child, and I can't blame you for that because you *are* a child. However, I want you to understand something. I warned you about taking care of your hamster because I didn't want to see *you* get hurt. It was to keep you from feeling like you do today that made me urge you to do your job properly. Now, there will be many other times when I will warn you and teach you and urge you to do something, and I'll also be doing that to keep you from being hurt by life. It is very important for you to see me as your friend, and when I tell you to do something, it is because I love you and can see dangers that you don't see. If you'll learn to listen to what I say, you'll have fewer times like today when you are so sad.'

My response to Danae's behaviour was dictated by the matter of her *intention*. She did not deliberately defy me and she deserved no punishment. Likewise, every parent should know his child well enough to make an instantaneous appraisal of this important factor, reacting accordingly.

(2) *How can I teach my fourteen-year-old the value of money?*

One good technique is to give him enough cash to meet a particular need, and then let him manage it. You can begin by offering a weekly food allowance to be spent in school. If he squanders the total on a weekend date, then it becomes his responsibility to either work for his lunches or go hungry. This is the cold reality he will face in later life, and it will not harm him to experience the lesson while still an adolescent.

I should indicate that this principle has been known to backfire, occasionally. A physician friend of mine has four daughters and he provides each one with an annual clothing allowance when they turn twelve years of age. It then becomes the girls' responsibility to budget their money for the garments that will be needed throughout the year. The last child to turn twelve, however, was not quite mature enough to handle the assignment. She celebrated her twelfth birthday by buying an expensive coat, which cut deeply into her available capital. The following spring, she exhausted her funds totally and wore shredded stockings, holey panties, and frayed dresses for the last three months of the year. It was difficult for her parents not to intervene, but they had the courage to let her learn this valuable lesson about money management.

Perhaps your son has never learned the value of money because it comes too easily. Anything in abundant supply becomes rather valueless. I would suggest that you restrict the pipeline and maximise the responsibility required in all expenditures.

(3) *We have a very flighty, bouncy, eight-year-old boy who cringes at the thought of work. His room is always a disaster area*

and he can sit and look at a job for hours without finishing it. How can we teach him to be more responsible?

Your son has a lot of company among eight-year-olds, most of whom get depressed over the very thought of work. Nevertheless, it is not too early to begin teaching him the meaning of self-discipline. I would suggest that you follow this plan:

(1) Early tomorrow morning, sit down with your son and tell him that you are going to begin teaching him how to work, because that is one of your jobs as a parent. Perhaps you will want to read him Proverbs 6:6–11 (LIVING BIBLE) where the value of work is described.

(2) Take him on a tour of his pigpen, showing him how messy he's been. All of this discussion is to be done without finger-wagging and accusations. It's just a matter of fact that the time has come to learn something new.

(3) List and post his daily jobs in his room. Spell out exactly what will be expected from him. Let him help select the jobs he will assume, equalling about one hour of work per day.

(4) For a confirmed goof-off, you will need to capitalise on every ounce of motivational power that can possibly be generated. Therefore, you must make use of the two things that 'move' kids: give him something to gain for doing the job right and something to lose for doing it wrong. The greater the distance between these two alternatives, the more willing he will be to accept his new responsibility. For example, I would construct an eight-inch thermometer as illustrated on the next page.

Down the left-hand side is the rate at which he will be paid for his work. Set the fee at whatever level is appropriate for a

child his age. Down the right-hand side is listed the time
factor, or number of hours worked. Each day, Junior fills in
the thermometer with a yellow or red pen, moving upward
towards a set goal. At the top is a picture of the objective,
whether it be a new phonograph record, a fishing reel, or
anything that the child wants badly.

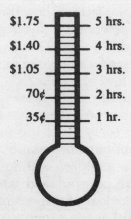

$1.75	5 hrs.
$1.40	4 hrs.
$1.05	3 hrs.
70¢	2 hrs.
35¢	1 hr.

For many irresponsible children, a second system must
accompany the first: there must be a reason not to reject the
offer (making use of both positive and negative reinforcement). To accomplish this purpose, tell your son: 'I have
worked out this thermometer plan to help you enjoy working,
because I don't want you to be miserable. But you don't have
the choice of accepting or rejecting it. One way or the other, I
am going to teach you how to work. If I don't do that, I will
fail in one of my most important jobs as a parent. So here is
our bargain. Your Saturdays are entirely free. You don't
have to do any work on Saturday, provided you complete
your jobs properly during the five weekdays. Each day that
you fail to do the things on your list, though, will be made up
on Saturday without pay. You see, if you do nothing five days
a week, you'll owe me five hours of free labour on Saturday. If
you get your work done all week, you get paid and Saturday
is yours. You choose which way it will be.'
Three things are essential to make this system

work. The absence of any one of the three will blow the entire game: (1) Don't nag and plead and push. The responsibility is his, not yours. One simple reminder might be appropriate, but the goal is to get him to do something on his own initiative. Discuss this in the beginning. (2) When he fails without excuse, be hard-nosed about the Saturday make-up time. That should be an extremely painful experience. If you fold up at this point and fail to follow through, you've lost the future motivational power from this negative reinforcement. You'll probably need it! (3) Make sure the goal at the top of the thermometer is something your son wants badly. Once he earns it, get it for him immediately.

There will be those who will oppose this kind of structured programme for a child, preferring that he work for the sheer love of work. I wish every child was noble enough to carry responsibility without outside pressure or reward. The truth of the matter is some children will do nothing for eighteen years unless they are programmed into a structure having only one way out: the door of responsiblity. If you have such a child, you must either plan such a programme or resign yourself to his sloppy procrastination.

Strategy No. 9

PREPARE FOR ADOLESCENCE

Now we turn to the heartburn and indigestion known as adolescence. I would be hard pressed to say whether the stresses of the teen years are more difficult for the youngster or for the other members of his family; this period of life offers something painful for everybody. But there are ways to minimise its impact, and this section will present suggestions towards that end.

The primary reason adolescence is so distressing is because the youngsters do not fully understand what is happening to them. Many of their fears, anxieties, and discouragements could be obviated by a simple instructional programme. Therefore I have long recommended that parents make a point of preparing their preteenagers for the events that are bound to follow. During the child's tenth year, or certainly no later than the eleventh, it would be wise for the knowledgable parent to schedule a weekend trip with that one child; they should go to the beach or the mountains or a local resort where they will not be disturbed. It would probably be best for fathers to talk to sons and mothers to teach their daughters, although the opposite sexes may communicate better in individual families. Those three days together would then be devoted to an explanation of the adolescent experience. Their conversations would involve much more than the laughable birds-and-bees talk, which usually degenerates to a tension-filled, sweaty-palmed discussion about reproductive facts which the kid had known for at least three years. Rather, I am recommending that parents present a carefully planned panorama of the physical, emotional, and social changes which are rapidly approaching.

It is further recommended that careful notes be taken during the course of the weekend. The parent should write down each point he has made regarding the remarkable changes that will be occurring in the child's body, the new demands that will be placed on him socially, the tension that is likely to develop between generations, and how it is all a part of growing up and becoming independent. A list should be made of the misconceptions which are so common to teenagers and the areas of greatest concern. They should pause briefly to discuss the spiritual confusion which often occurs in adolescence, and in conclusion, focus on occupational and career choices the child must eventually make. The purpose for dutifully recording the text of these conversations is that the child is not going to remember much of what he was told. The words of his parent will quietly slip away during the years that follow. But the notes are to be kept in an accessible place until they are needed. Several years later, when Junior is discouraged and distressed and rejected and lovesick and emotional and anxious, the paper should be retrieved. Being careful to time the follow-up discussion properly, the paper is again reviewed with the adolescent. His parent can then say, 'You see, each thing that you're experiencing was anticipated several years ago. It was as predictable as that the sun will rise, for it is all a part of the transition from childhood to manhood (or woman-hood).' Then the parent points to the last item on the final page, which reads, 'Normality *will* return!' He is told that just as surely as these upsettings events were accurately predicted, their end can also be forecast with equal certainty.

You see, if the trials of adolescence can be viewed by a youngster as a temporary phase through which everyone must pass, then his distress is more tolerable. But the natural inclination of an immature mind is to see today as forever. 'My situation is awful and it will never change. There is no way out. There are no solutions and no one understands.' These explosive thoughts can be defused by a caring parent.

There is one hitch in the recommendation above. Before a parent can teach his child the details of adolescence, he must *know* the subject himself. Invariably when I have proposed this instructional programme to groups of parents, they have asked for more information regarding what the lessons should include. Therefore, the section which follows will be addressed primarily to that request. Intermingled with this description are related suggestions for the teen years. You may want to read some passages from this section to your child or use these recommendations to structure your own approach.

What Is Adolescence?

All of us are familiar with the term 'adolescence', yet its definition is frequently misunderstood. It is NOT a physical term, as such. It does not mean 'the time of life when a child matures sexually.' That is the definition of 'puberty'. Adolescence is a *cultural term*, meaning the age between childhood and adulthood in a particular society. It is the period of time when an individual neither has the privileges of childhood nor the freedom of adulthood.

The length of adolescence varies remarkably from one

society to another. Some primitive tribes, for example, have *no* adolescence at all. One day a pubescent boy or girl is treated as a child – allowed to play and expected to follow the wishes of his parents. The next day he undergoes the traditional rites of puberty – perhaps spending a night alone in the forest in pursuit of a mythical animal. When he returns home he is a full-fledged adult. He fights in battles, works with the other adults, and enjoys the status and respect of maturity. There is, then, no in-between phase for these young people.

By contrast, we in the western world have the longest period of adolescence in the history of mankind, and herein lies much of the related discontent. For an intolerably long period of time, our children are without status and respect. They resent their plight, and I can understand their frustration. For the fifteen-year-old, everything 'adult' is forbidden. He can't drive. He can't marry. He can't enlist. He can't borrow. He can't drink (legally). He can't make his own decisions. He can't vote. He can't join a labour union. And his sexual desires are denied gratification during this period of greatest excitation. In fact, his only alternative is to continue in school whether he likes it or not. We as adults know it must be this way, yet the teenager often interprets our prohibitions as evidence of disrespect.

This in-between age usually lasts as long as the individual remains financially dependent upon his parents. Thus, in some cases, a twenty-five-year-old graduate student has not been granted complete adult status by his parental benefactors. Ordinarily, however, adolescence lasts from age thirteen to twenty-one in males and from twelve to twenty-one in females (terminating earlier if marriage occurs or if education is interrupted). Obviously, nine or ten years is a long time to be disenfranchised by a society, accounting for some of the rebellion of that period.

Knowing that adolescents often chafe under their lack of status in the adult world, I would offer this very important suggestion to the parents of a teenager: treat him with genuine respect and dignity. Let your manner convey your acceptance of him as an individual, even aiming your conversation a year or two above his head. Does this mean you have to pussyfoot with him when he has defied your authority or overstepped reasonable boundaries? Certainly not. It is possible to treat a child respectfully, even when punishment is necessary. In fact, during my years as a schoolteacher – at times seeing 225 teenagers in my classroom each day – I learned that youngsters will tolerate all sorts of rules and restrictions, provided you don't assault their egos. But if you make them feel childish and foolish, brace yourself for wrath and hostility. Much of the strife between generations could be eliminated if the relationship was mixed generously with mutual respect.

Let's examine, now, the other subjects which should be discussed with a child during the months immediately prior to adolescence.

Adolescence Is an Age of Dramatic Physical Change

Every preteenager should be informed of the rapid changes which are about to occur within his body. For the adult who has ever lost sleep over an unidentified lump or other suspicious symptom, it is easy to imagine how a youngster feels when everything goes haywire all at once. I have found that uninformed teenagers fall into two broad categories: (1) The first group didn't know the physical changes were coming and are worried sick by what they see happening; (2) the second group is aware that certain features are supposed to appear and are anxious because the changes are late in arriving. Whether your child is voicing his fears or not, it is likely that he is asking himself scores of tense questions: Does this pain in my breasts mean I have cancer? Why do I feel tired all the time? The older boys have hair down below; why don't I? Am I normal? Will I always look like a baby? Why do I have cramps and pain in my stomach? Could I bleed to death? What is happening to my voice? The doubts and fears are endless, yet they could be avoided by healthy, confident parental instruction. Listed below are some of the subjects which should be discussed in anticipation of adolescence:

(1) Rapid growth will occur, sapping energy and strength for a while. The teenager will actually need more sleep and better nutrition than when he was younger.

(2) Tell your child that his body will quickly change to that of an adult. His sex organs will become more mature and will be surrounded by pubic hair. (For males, stress this point: the size of the penis is of no physical importance. Many boys worry tremendously about having a smaller organ, but that has *nothing* to do with fathering a child or sexual satisfaction as an adult. For girls, breast development can also be discussed in the same manner.)

(3) The full details of the menstrual cycle must be made clear to your daughter before her first period. It is a terrifying thing for a girl to experience this aspect of maturity without forewarning. Many books and films are available to help explain this developmental milestone, and should be used. The most important parental responsibility at this point is to convey confidence, optimism, and excitement regarding menstruation, rather than saying sadly, 'This is the cross you must bear as a woman.'

(4) It is most important that the timing of puberty be discussed with your children, for herein lies *much* grief and distress. This period of heightened sexual development may occur as early as twelve or as late as nineteen years of age in boys and from ten to seventeen in girls. Thus, it may arrive seven years earlier in some children that in others! And the youngsters who develop very early or very late usually face some upsetting psychological problems. There are four extremes which should be considered:

The Late-Maturing Boy. This little fellow knows perfectly well that he is still a baby while his friends have grown up. He picks up the telephone and the operator calls him 'ma'am'! What an insult! He's very interested in athletics at this age, but he can't compete with the larger, stronger boys. He gets teased in the locker room about his sexual immaturity, and his self-esteem nose-dives. And adding insult to injury, he is actually shorter than most of the girls for a couple of years! (They have had their growth spurt and he has not.) He fears that there is something drastically wrong in his case, but he dares not mention his thoughts to anyone. It's too embarrassing. This prepubertal child can often be the worst troublemaker in the school, for he has many things to prove about his doubtful manhood.

The Late-Maturing Girl. Life is no easier for the girl whose internal clock is on the slow side. She looks down at her flat chest and then glances at her busty friends. For two or three years, her girl friends have been sharing confidences about menstruation, but she can't participate in the discussions. She has been nicknamed 'baby face' by the gang, and in fact, she does look about eight years old. Remembering the role physical attractiveness plays in self-esteem, the reader can see that inferiority can overwhelm the late developer, even if he or she *is* attractively arranged. And unless someone tells them otherwise, they are likely to conclude that they will never grow up.

The Early Maturing Girl. If it is disadvantageous to be late in maturing, one would think that the opposite would be emotionally healthy. Not so. Since girls tend to develop sexually one or two years before boys, on an average, the girl who enters puberty before other girls is miles ahead of everybody else her age. Physical strength offers her no real advantages in our society, and it is simply not acceptable to be boy-crazy at ten years of age. For two or three uncomfortable years, the early maturing girl is out of step with all her age mates.

The Early Maturing Boy. By contrast, the early maturing boy is blessed with a great social advantage. He is strong at a time when power is worshipped by his peers, and his confidence soars as his athletic successes are publicised. His early development places him on a par with the girls in his class, who are also awakening sexually. Thus, he has the field all to himself for a year or two. Research confirms that the early maturing boy is more frequently emotionally stable, confident and socially accepted than other boys. It also shows that he is more likely to be more successful in later adult life, as well.

In the discussion of these extremes with your preteenager, assure him that it is 'normal' for some youngsters to be early or late in developing. It does not mean that anything is wrong with his body. If indeed he is a late bloomer, he will need additional reassurance and encouragement in the years ahead. Finally, an attempt should be made at the time of this conversation to open the door of communication regarding the fears and anxieties associated with physical growth and development.

Incidentally, I should mention one more aspect of adolescent physiology before moving on. Statistical records indicate that our children are growing taller today than in the past, probably resulting from better nutrition, medicine, exercise, rest, and recreation. And this additional stature has produced an interesting consequence: sexual maturity is occurring at younger and younger ages. Apparently, puberty in a particular child is 'turned on' when he reaches a certain level of growth; therefore, when environmental circumstances propel him upward at a faster rate, he becomes sexually mature much earlier. For example, in 1850, the average of the menarche (first menstruation) in Norwegian girls was 17.0 years of age; in 1950, it was 13.0. The average age of puberty had dropped 4 years in that one century. In the United States, the average age of the menarche dropped from 14.2 in 1900 to 12.9 in 1950. More recent figures indicate the average has now dropped closer to 12½ years of age! Thus, a portion of the trend towards younger dating and sexual awareness is a result of this physiological mechanism. I suppose we could slow it down by taking poorer care of our children – but I doubt if that idea will gain much sympathy.

Adolescence Is an Age of Inferiority

Your preadolescent youngster should be told the meaning of inferiority and warned about its impact. He should understand that inadequacy is an unnecessary cross that *most* adolescents carry, even though they seem to be happy and contented. There is no greater service that a parent can perform for his preteenager than to 'defuse' the self-worth crisis before it arrives, making it appear universal and temporary. 'Nearly every teenager feels inadequate,' he should be told, 'and you may go through this stage, too. But if you do, remember that it is part of the process of growing up and doesn't really have much to do with genuine self-worth.'

I believe that the false values described in this book should be discussed openly with your youngster. You see, if he knows where the pain is likely to occur, he can build defences against it. By contrast, the lonely little fellow who is never informed about inferiority gets hit from behind by an awful gloom which springs without warning from the adolescent darkness. It need not be so.

Adolescence Is an Age of Conformity

The pressure to follow the whims of the group (called the herd instinct) is never so great as it is during the adolescent years. This drive may be all-consuming to a teenager when *any* deviation fron the 'in' behaviour is a serious breach of etiquette. And there is tyranny in this pressure. If the group says flared pants are out, woe be to the boy who doesn't get the message soon enough. If a girl talks or walks funny, she may be the object of scorn throughout her day. Therefore, each teenager knows that safety from ridicule can only be found by remaining precisely on the chalk line of prevailing opinion. For the youngster whose emotional needs and self-doubt are the greatest dare not run the risk of defying the will of the majority on even the most trivial matter.

The influence of peer pressure is best illustrated by a study of teenagers conducted by Ruth W. Berenda. She and her associates brought ten adolescents into a room and told them that they were going to study their perception (how well they could see). To test this ability, they planned to hold up cards on which three lines were drawn. The lines were marked A, B, and C and were of three different lengths, as illustrated below. Line A was the longest on some cards, while lines B or C were longer on others. As the cards were held before the class, the researcher would point to A, B, and C consecutively, asking the students to raise their hands when the pointer was directed at the longest line.

The instructions were simple and were repeated. 'Raise your hand when we point to the longest line.' What one student didn't know, however, is that the other nine had been brought in early and told to vote for the second longest line. The purpose was to test the effect of group pressure on that lonely individual.

A ————————	A ————————————	A —————————
B ———————	B ——————	B ————
C —————	C ———	C ————————

The experiment began with nine teenagers voting for the wrong line. The stooge would typically glance around, frown in confusion, and slip his hand up with the group. The instructions were repeated and the next card was raised. Time after time, the self-conscious stooge would sit there saying a short line is longer than a long line, simply because he lacked the courage to challenge the group. This remarkable conformity occurred in about seventy-five per cent of the cases, and was true of small children and high-school students as well. Berenda concluded that, 'Some people had rather be president than right,' which is certainly an accurate assessment.

This same desire to look and think like other teenagers causes problems for those who can't conform. I knew a blind, fifteen-year-old girl who refused to admit she had a handicap. She would not accept the help of a special teacher provided by the school, and her parents could not even get her to use a white cane. To thump along the corridor marked her as different from her peers, and she couldn't tolerate the distinction. I watched one day as she walked to her next class with her head erect, as though she knew where she was going. Before I could stop her, she walked straight into a post. Even this experience was insufficient to make her use a device which other teenagers did not need.

Similarly, I worked with the parents of a second-grade boy having a hearing problem. He simply would not let them put a hearing aid in his ear. He had rather be deaf than different. Truly, conformity is a powerful drive in children of all ages. And we adults had better get on board, too! We can't even comb our hair the way we wish because everyone knows 'the wethead is dead!' What could be more humiliating than walking around town with your hair oil glistening in the sunshine. Awful thought!

Before I leave the subject, I should mention the fact that adolescent peer-group pressure accounts for some of the strain between generations and a lessening of parental influence during this time, I have seen parents get 'hurt' because their developing teenager suddenly seemed embarrassed to be with them. 'I went to the door of death to bring the kid into the world,' a mother may say, 'and then he grows up to be ashamed to even be seen in my presence.' She should understand that teenagers are engulfed by a tremendous desire to be adults, and they resent anything which implies that they are still children. When they are seen with 'Mommie and Daddy' on a Friday night, for example, their humiliation is almost unbearable. They are not really ashamed of their parents; they are embarrassed by the adult-baby role that was more appropriate in prior years. Parents would do well to accept this healthy aspect of growing up without becoming defensive about it.

My own mother understood this process well, and she made use of it for her own purposes. When I was in the ninth grade, I suddenly discovered that it was much more fun to fool around in school than to work and cooperate. So for that one year, I played and laughed and irritated my teachers. But I didn't fool my mother. I don't know how she got her information, but she knew that I had gone giddy. One day she sat me down and said, 'I know what you're doing in school. I know you're playing and causing trouble. However, I have decided not to do anything about it. I'm not going to punish you or threaten you or even call the principal. *But if the school ever calls me*, I am going to go with you the very next day. I'll follow you to all your classes and sit in the seat beside you. I will hold your hand and tag around after you throughout the day. Just remember my promise.'

Believe me, friends and neighbours, that straightened me out quick! It would have been social suicide for my big momma to follow me down the halls of Adolescent High School. Beat me, but don't come to school with me! I'm sure my teachers wondered why there was such a remarkable improvement in my behaviour during the last half of my fourteenth year.

In summary, it is important for your preteenager to know about group pressure before it reaches its peak. Someday he may be sitting in a car with four friends who decide to shoot some heroin. Your preparation is no guarantee that he will have the courage to stand alone in that crucial moment, but his knowledge of peer influence could provide the independence to do what is right. I would, therefore, recommend that this entire section on conformity be read and discussed with your ten- or eleven-year-old.

Adolescence Is an Age of Confusion

A small child is told what to think during his formative years. He is subjected to all the attitudes, biases, and beliefs of his parents, which is right and proper. They are fulfilling their God-given responsibility to guide and train him. However, there must come a moment when all of these concepts and ideas are examined by the individual, and either adopted as true or rejected as false. If that personal evaluation never comes, then the adolescent fails to span the gap between 'What I've been told' versus 'What I believe'. This is one of the most important bridges leading from childhood to adulthood.

It is common, then, for a teenager to question the veracity of the indoctrination he has received. He may ask himself, 'Is there really a God? Does He know me? Do I believe in the values my parents have taught? Do I want what they want for my life? Have they misled me in any way? Does my experience contradict what I've been taught?' For a period of years beginning during adolescence and continuing into the twenties, this intensive self-examination is conducted.

Your preadolescent should be forewarned about the distress he may experience later during this period of questioning. It is truly an age of confusion, for nothing can be considered absolute or certain. Furthermore, you, his parent, should also brace yourself for this experience. It is very difficult to sit on the sidelines and watch your child scrutinise the values to which your life has been dedicated. The process will be much less painful for everyone, however, if both generations realise that the soul-searching is a normal, necessary part of growing up.

Adolescence Is an Age of Identity Formation

Much has been written about the 'search for identity', but I doubt if your ten-year-old has read much of that literature. Consequently, you will need to talk to him about what it means to know himself. The child with a good sense of

identity is acquainted with his own goals, strengths, weak-
nesses, desires, hopes, and dreams. He could sit down and
write a paper entitled, 'Who am I?' without bogging down on
the first paragraph. A child who has been given a meaningful
self-awareness by his parents and teachers knows where he's
going and how he expects to get there. He is a fortunate
individual in this day of grey, indistinct self-awareness.

I would like to describe a less fortunate young fellow whom
I have known professionally. You know him, too, for he lives
in every neighbourhood, attends every school, is a member of
every church. Perhaps five million carbon copies are walking
the streets of America today, with slight variation. This
teenager, whom I'll call John, was neither the first nor the
last child born into his family, making him merely one of a
group (or a crowd) at home. His parents were extremely
busy during his early childhood and their effort went into the
necessities of living. They read to John very rarely and never
viewed him with any distinct pride. They just let him grow
up on his own. His physical features were not grotesque, but
he was certainly no Prince Charming either; he was merely
'ho hum' to look at.

When John toddled off to school, he immediately had
trouble learning to read. He couldn't explain why, but the
message didn't get through. He didn't actually fail but his
academic work was hardly worth remembering. His teachers
thought of him, not as an individual, but as a member of that
thirty or forty per cent of uninspired students who have to
work harder to achieve the same result. In fact, it was easy to
forget that Johnny was even there.

As John came through elementary and junior-high school,
he never excelled in anything. He did not star in Little
League. He never learned to make model airplanes. He
rarely had more than one or two casual friends at a time. He
didn't win the safety award in school or the American
Freedoms badge from the local service club. He was not
chosen class president. He did not learn to work in his
father's carpentry shop. He never did anything for his
parents to brag to the neighbours about. I suppose his

childhood was invested primarily in television and comic books and tree-climbing.

Then little Johnny suddenly became Big John during his fifteenth year. Pimples and blackheads besieged his head, and wouldn't you know, his nose developed a slight hook to the left. The boys considered him a bore and the girls could look right through him without noticing that he was there at all. He went out for basketball in the fall, but the coach was busy working with the talented boys. He quit the next day 'because it wasn't inneresting.' His posture was poor and his manners were appalling. And he had never given one serious thought to the future beyond high school.

In short, John and all the others he symbolises, reaches his sixteenth year totally lacking in personal identity except for a nebulous self-disgust. He does not know who he is, what he wants, or where he is going. It is at this point that his vulnerability to social suggestion reaches a peak. Any group which comes along and offers a sense of identity may be adopted in toto. Consider the motorcycle gang, the Hell's Angels, for example. They can offer John everything he lacks. In return for his allegiance they can give him a bevy of friends, a sense of power, an accepted 'in group' language, the kind of clothes to wear (leather jacket, boots, etc.), the form of transportation to use (motorcycles), and a complete set of amoral values and attitudes. In one stroke, they can take a meaningless, bland teenager and instil in him a definite, prescribed (though anti-social) identity.

It is your job as a parent to provide your child with a healthy identity during the formative years in the home. How is this accomplished? By helping him recognise his own strengths and interests. By teaching him what to believe and how to behave. And perhaps most importantly, by giving him compensating skills, described in Strategy No. 4. If you don't do this job, as the song says, 'Somebody else will!'

Adolescence Is an Age of Fluctuating Emotions and Personality Changes

The adolescent experience is typically characterised by

emotional 'highs' and 'lows', operating in cyclical fashion. These mood fluctuations can be disconcerting to other family members, who must learn to live with alternating depression, elation, and everything in between. Perhaps more distressing is the inconstancy of maturity during this time. One day a fifteen-year-old may think and act like a full-grown man; the next day he is a child all over again.

If each family member is taught to recognise the fluctuating personality pattern as 'normal', they might find it easier to live with an emotional, excitable, impressionable, erratic, idealistic, flighty, daydreaming romanticist known as an adolescent.

Adolescence Is an Age of Sexual Fascination and Fear

Perhaps the most important conversation to be held in preparation for adolescence will deal with the sexual awakening which your child is about to experience. If you have been doing your job properly through the years, this final presentation will represent a review of the matters you and he have discussed many times before. It is appropriately called a 'final' presentation because it may be your last open interchange on this delicate subject. Whereas most topics can be approached directly with a ten-year-old, he will probably be resentful and embarrassed by the same conversation about three years later. After a child undergoes the emotional, hormonal, and anatomical changes of puberty, your job as his primary sex educator will probably be a thing of the past. In a sense, then, the prepubertal discussion about sex is similar to a coach giving advice to his players immediately prior to the big game. He says, 'Remember what I've taught you, and don't forget the rules of the game. Let's go over the fundamentals one more time.' The coach knows that after the game begins, there will be little time or opportunity for further instruction.

This vital discussion about sex is much too important to attempt without planning and forethought. In fact, all along through the formative years, spontaneous opportunities appear for which your preparation must already be invested. It may be helpful to review the checklist of ten subjects, cited below, in preparing for the discussions I've recommended. You should have a good notion of what you will say about each of these topics:

(1) The role of intercourse in marriage
(2) Male and female anatomy and physiology
(3) Pregnancy and the birth process
(4) Nocturnal emission ('wet dreams')
(5) Masturbation
(6) Guilt and sexual fantasy
(7) Menstruation
(8) Morality and responsibility in sex
(9) Venereal disease
(10) Secondary sex characteristics which will be brought about by glandular changes – pubic hair, general sexual development, increasing interest in sex, etc.

Since few parents can claim to be experts in sex education, I would strongly recommend that they adopt the appropriate motto of the Boy Scouts of America: 'Be Prepared!' (The scope of this book does not permit a complete discussion of the ten items presented above. It is suggested that parents consult *Sex Is a Parent Affair* by Letha Scanzoni or other worthwhile books on sex education.)

One further matter should be mentioned before leaving this topic. There is often a very important link between irresponsible sexual activity and low self-esteem, which underscores the urgency of teaching proper attitudes and behaviour with regard to the opposite sex. It has been shown repeatedly that adolescents with the greatest sense of inferiority are often the most vulnerable to sexual experimentation and exploitation. Two sociologists, John Gagnon and William Simon, have found that the least popular students are most likely to be sexually promiscuous. Having never felt social acceptance, they leap at the first person who offers affection in exchange for intimate privileges. However, those same inadequate youngsters – especially the girls – soon find that their sexual availability brings only a momentary sort of attention, followed by more unhappiness. Dr. Emery Breitner agrees. He studied adult 'swingers' who engage in wife swapping, extramarital sex, etc. Most of his subjects openly admitted that they were looking for love, companionship, approval, and acceptance. His conclusion: 'Promiscuous people are "love addicts" who want to be loved all the time and be reassured that they are loved. For them the only way to achieve this is sex.'

Dorothy Corkille Briggs, writing in her book, *Your Child's Self-Esteem*, stated it succinctly:

> The evidence suggests that the best insurance against indiscriminate sexual behaviour when the herd instinct runs high in adolescence – when sexual urges are intense – is a high degree of personal worth. A sense of personal value insulates a youngster from selling himself short and lessens interest in irresponsible sexual behaviour.

Obviously, we as parents need to work on both sides of the equation: reduce the inferiority and teach healthy sexual attitudes simultaneously.

Adolescence Is an Age of Increasing Independence

It will be very helpful to describe the 'break-away' process which is about to occur to your preadolescent. I would suggest that he be given a description similar to the statement below:

> Paul, you were born into our family as a completely helpless, dependent infant. Throughout your childhood, your mother and I have led you and guided you and taught you what we believe is right. But we won't always have a parent-child relationship as we do now. Within about ten years, you will probably be living

away from home, earning your own money, and making your own decisions. You will become an adult, and will probably have a family of your own to care for. Sometimes this process of growing up and becoming responsible for your own life puts a great strain on a family. Many times a child wants to grow up too fast for his own good — making decisions he isn't ready for — and his parents have to hold back and slow him down. Other teenagers want to go on living at home, taking food and clothing and shelter from their parents, but they don't want to be told what to do any more. These tensions put a crunch on the whole family, sometimes making loved ones angry at each other.

The reason I'm telling you this is because I want you to understand what is happening if this kind of feeling comes between us. It won't last forever, and in fact, it can be avoided if we keep talking to each other and trying to understand the other side. There are, then, several things that I want you to remember:

(1) I am going to give you a little more freedom each year, as I think you are ready for it. There will be certain things that you will have to accept as long as you are living at home and you will not always like the rules that are established here. However, your mother and I will gradually allow you to make more of your own decisions as you grow older.

(2) As your freedom increases, so will your level of responsibility. I'll expect you to carry more and more of the family work load, and you'll earn a greater percentage of your own spending money. This responsibility will help prepare you for successful adult living.

(3) If you ever feel we are being unfair with you during the teenage years, you are free to come to us and express your feelings. You can say what you really think, and I'll consider your viewpoint. However, I will never honour a temper tantrum. If you slam

doors and pout and scream, as many teenagers do when they get upset, you'll find my ears completely closed.

(4) Above all, remember that you are tremendously loved, and everything that we do will be motivated by that affection. And even if we get upset with each other in the years to come, that deep love will always be there. I look forward to these last years you'll have at home. Before we know it, you'll be gone and we'll only have memories of these happy days together. Let's make the most of them as a family.

Such a conversation should serve to pacify at least part of the rebellion that often accompanies the adolescent experience.

Summary

In conclusion, adolescence can be a more tranquil experience for the family that prepares properly for its arrival. To ignore its approaching onset, however, is like riding up a roller coaster for the first time, not knowing what awaits at the top of the incline. The trip down can be harrowing for everyone on board. There is a better way.

IMPORTANT NOTE: It has become obvious that many parents do not feel capable of conducting the preadolescent training session which I've described in this section. They are concerned about sex education and the other difficult subjects which must be conveyed. In an attempt to assist with this task, I have recorded an album of six cassette tapes, entitled 'Preparing for Adolescence'. Each of the topics mentioned in this section is described in conversational style, to be heard by parent and child together. These records are accompanied by a book, also entitled *Preparing for Adolescence*, a workbook, and two tapes for parents. These materials

are designed to stimulate further discussion and interaction between generations. They are available in book-
stores, or by writing to 'Preparing for Adolescence', Box
952, Temple City, California 91780 USA.

Questions and Answers

(1) *We have a fourteen-year-old daughter who is going through
the worst of what you've described. She feels ugly and tremendously inferior. She hates herself and everyone else, too. Her
personality is sour and she is depressed most of the time. It is
obviously too late to 'prepare her' for adolescence; she is drowning
in it right now! What can we possibly do to help her?*

Yours is the toughest job in parenthood. The danger is
that your child may seek to deal with her feelings in ways that
bring her greater trouble, such as through drugs, or an early
marriage, or by dropping out of school, or by running away,
or identification with an antisocial group of some type. Your
love and subtle guidance are more important to her right
now than at any other time in her life, though magic solutions
are rather scarce.

First, when the despair is as intense as you describe, I
strongly recommend that you seek to place your child in a
group therapy class. Teenagers have such remarkable influence on each other that they can help pull themselves out
of an emotional ditch. Furthermore, it will be refreshing for
your daughter to hear, firsthand, that other teen-agers have
exactly the same feelings and fears that she has experienced.
And finally, there is great emotional release to be found in
being able to talk about her frustrations and anxieties within
the accepting atmosphere of the group. Your local high
school counselling office should be able to help you locate an
appropriate group in your area.

Secondly, I would suggest that you make the following
suggestion to your troubled daughter:

Sometime when you are all alone, it would be a good
idea to sit down and list all the things you don't like

about yourself. Be sure you have a big stack of blank paper because you're probably going to need it. No one will ever see this paper but you, unless you reveal it, so you can afford to be completely honest. Write down all the things that bother you, and then place check marks by the matters which worry you the most.

When this has been done, then come back through the list and think about each item. Give your greatest creative thought to what might be done to change the things you don't like. If you wish, you might share the paper with your pastor or counsellor or parent or someone in whom you have confidence; that person can then help you map out a plan for improvement. You'll feel better for having faced your problems, and you might even find genuine solutions to some of the troublesome matters.

Now we come to an important step. The key to mental health is being able to accept what you cannot change. After you've done what you can to deal with your problems, I feel you should take the paper on which the most painful items are written, and burn it in a private ceremony before God. Commit your life to Him once more – strengths and weaknesses – good points and bad – asking Him to take what you have and bless it. After all, He created the entire universe from nothing, and He can make something beautiful out of your life. The words of Bill Gaither's song express this thought perfectly:

> Something beautiful, something good,
> All my confusion, He understood.
> All I had to offer Him was brokenness and strife,
> But He made something beautiful of my life.

(2) *Our teenage daughter has become extremely modest in recent months, demanding that even her sisters leave her room when she's dressing. I think this is silly, don't you?*

No, I would suggest that you honour her requests for privacy. Her sensitivity is probably caused by an awareness that her body is changing, and she is embarrassed by recent developments (or the lack of them). This is likely to be a temporary phase and you should not oppose her in it.

(3) *Must I act like a teenager myself, in dress, language, tastes, and manner, in order to show my adolescent that I understand him?*

Emphatically not. There is something disgusting about a thirty-five-year-old 'adolescent has-been.' It wasn't necessary for you to crawl on the floor and throw temper tantrums in order to understand your two-year-old; likewise, you can reveal an empathy and acceptance of the teen years without becoming an anachronistic teenybopper yourself. In fact, the very reason for your adolescent's unique manner and style is to display an identity separate from yours. You'll turn him off quickly by invading his identity, leading him to conclude, 'Mom tries so hard, but I wish she'd grow up!' Besides, he will still need an authority figure on occasion, and you've got the job!

(4) *I have read about the 'unisex movement', which holds that the differences between men and women should be minimised, whether in work, play, or fashion. Would you comment on this, particularly with reference to teaching traditional male and female roles to boys and girls. Do you think boys should be made to do girls' work, and vice versa?*

The trend towards the blending of masculine and feminine roles is well ingrained in America at this time. Women smoke cigars and wear pants. Men splash on perfume and don jewellery. There is little sexual identity seen in their hair length, manner, interests, or occupations, and the trend is ever more in this direction. Such similarity between men and women causes great confusion in the minds of children with regard to their own sex-role identity. They have no distinct models to imitate and are left to grope for the appropriate behaviour and attitudes.

There can be little doubt that this blurring of roles is contributing to the homosexual epidemic and related sexual confusion which we now face. Historically, unisex attitudes have preceded the disintegration of societies which drifted in that direction. Dr. Charles Winick, professor of anthropology at City University of New York, studied 2,000 different cultures, and found 55 which were characterised by sexual ambiguity. Not one has survived. Dr. Winick feels America's future is at stake in this issue, and I am inclined to agree.

In regard to our children, I *firmly* believe in the value of teaching traditional male and female roles during the early years. To remove this prescribed behaviour for a child is to further damage his sense of identity, which needs all the help it can get. The masculine and feminine roles are taught through clothing, close identification with the parent of the same sex, and to some degree, through the kind of work required, and in the selection of toys provided for play. I am not suggesting that we panic over tomboy tendencies in our girls or that we demand he-man behaviour from our boys. Nor is it unacceptable for a boy to wash the dishes or a girl to clean the garage. We should, on the other hand, gently nudge our children in the direction of their appropriate sex role.

My answer to your question will meet with opposition among those who want to see the differences disappear between men and women. I strongly disagree. According to my understanding of the divine plan, as explicitly stated in the Bible, the two sexes are ordained for specific masculine and feminine roles which cannot be ignored without painful consequences. Men and women are *equal* but not equivalent! That is, they have equal human worth but are designed for distinctly different responsibilities. It is my prayer that America will not abandon that inspired purpose at this delicate point in its history.

(5) *What causes homosexuality?*

Homosexuality has many causes, in the same way that a fever may occur from different sources. However, as a generalisation, it can be said that homosexuality results from an unhappy home life, usually involving confusion in sexual identity.

(6) *What is the most common home environment of a future homosexual?*

Again, conditions vary tremendously, although the most common seems to be a home where the mother is dominating, overprotective, and possessive, while the father is rejecting and ridiculing of the child. The opposite situation occurs, too, where the mother rejects her son because he is a male.

(7) *Can homosexuality ever result from a single, traumatic experience?*

It happens, though not often. I worked with one homosexual teenager whose drunken father forced him to 'sleep' with his mother following a New Year's Eve party. His disgust for sex with women was easy to trace. Most cases are less obvious, however.

(8) *What can parents do to prevent this problem in their children?*

The best prevention is to strengthen their home life. Homosexuality rarely occurs in a loving home, where parents are reasonably well adjusted sexually, themselves. I don't think it is necessary to fear this unfortunate occurrence as a force beyond our control. If parents will provide a healthy, stable home environment, and not interfere with the child's appropriate sex role, then homosexuality is highly unlikely to occur in the younger set.

(9) *A recent book for parents contends that good sex education will reduce the incidence of promiscuity and sexual irresponsibility among teenagers. Do you agree?*

Of course not. Teenagers are sexually better informed today than at any time in human history, although the traditional boy-girl game seems to be as popular as ever. The assumption that physiological information will inhibit sexual activity is about as foolish as thinking an overweight glutton can be helped by understanding the biological process of eating. I am in favour of proper sex education for other reasons — but I have no illusions about its unique power to instil responsibility in adolescents. Morality, if it is valued, must be approached directly, rather than through the back doors of anatomy and physiology. Of much greater potency is a lifelong demonstration of morality in all its forms by parents whose very lives reveal their fidelity and commitment to one another.

(10) *You mentioned the need to help a child get acquainted with himself. How can you help him know his own interests, particularly in late adolescence when he is thinking of his occupational future?*

There is an excellent test available for this purpose. It is called the *Strong Vocational Interest Test*, and can be given by most high school counsellors. The cost is minimal, and the results correlate a teenager's interests with answers to the same 400 questions by successful members of 40 professions. The test is scored by a computer for less than five dollars and provides a well-rounded panorama of one's interests.

Strategy No. 10

A MESSAGE FOR DISCOURAGED ADULTS

Although the primary focus of this book is on the preventative measures against inferiority to be taken on behalf of small children by the home and school, we should pause, briefly, to comment on the similar problems of adulthood. As indicated in the first chapter, low self-esteem is extremely common among adults today, being particularly prevalent with American women. I simply cannot overemphasise this point. Virtually every woman I have counselled has expressed a poverty of inner confidence. This explains my answer to the gifted writer, Joyce Landorf, when she asked me the following question: 'What would you change about women in general, if you could wave some sort of magic wand?' My reply, now quoted in Mrs. Landorf's excellent book, *The Fragrance of Beauty*, was written with conviction:

> If I could write a prescription for the women of the world, it would provide each one of them with a healthy dose of self-esteem and personal worth (taken three times a day until the symptoms disappear). I have no doubt that this is their greatest need.

To verify my observation of widespread personal dissatisfaction by the gentle sex, I created a questionnaire entitled 'Sources of Depression Among Women' (mentioned briefly within Strategy No. 1). Ten items were listed, as illustrated below.

SOURCES OF DEPRESSION AMONG WOMEN

Please rank the following sources of depression according to their applicability in your life. Do not sign your name.

IRRITANT	YOUR RANK
1. Absence of *romantic* love in my marriage	————
2. In-law conflict	————
3. Low self-esteem	————
4. Problems with the children	————
5. Financial difficulties	————
6. Loneliness, isolation and boredom	————
7. Sexual problems in marriage	————
8. Menstrual and physiological problems	————
9. Fatigue and time pressure	————
10. Ageing	————

The questionnaire was administered to two groups of women, totalling about seventy-five individuals. Their average age was about thirty years, and all were middle-class wives and mothers. They were asked to mark their answers to the questionnaire in complete privacy, submitting the anonymous forms for tally. When the results were calculated, the first group had clearly indicated 'low self-esteem' as the most common source of depression, and the other group marked it a close second! These results were even more surprising, considering the fact that the participating women were primarily healthy, happily married, attractive young women who seemingly had everything to live for. Furthermore, most of them confessed to being members of the Christian faith. The conclusion from this questionnaire and related evidence is inescapable: inferiority and inadequacy have become constant companions of many, perhaps most, American women today. (The remaining results from the questionnaire are included in my book *What Wives Wish Their Husbands Knew About Women*, devoted to the needs of adults.)

While the incidence of overwhelming inferiority is probably lower in men than women, the problem is certainly not exclusively a feminine one. It has surfaced in places where it would be least expected. I was recently invited to conduct a lecture series for faculty and students at a seminary. It seemed appropriate that I talk to these future ministers about the subject of inferiority, since they would soon be dealing with many such problems in their own congregations. During the course of my first address, I relayed a story of 'Danny'. Danny was a distressed high-school student whose grief over his inadequacy became intolerable and eventually turned to anger. After I had spoken that day, I received the following anonymous letter:

Dear Dr. Dobson –
I am one of the 'Dannys' you spoke of in chapel today. Believe me, for I have experienced this for as long as I can remember. It is a miserable way to live.
Yes, I'm a student at the seminary, but that doesn't

make the problem any less acute. Through the years, particularly the last five, I have periodically gained a revived hope that somehow(?) this problem can be overcome – go away or something. Then to my great disappointment, I find it is still very much a part of me. That's when I lose hope of ever conquering it. I want to be a minister of the gospel and feel that this is God's will. *At the same time I am aware of the paralysing effect this deep problem has upon me.* I want so badly to be adequate so that I could better serve God and others.

I wish I could talk to with you, even for a short time. However, I realise your busy schedule. At any rate, thank you for coming to the seminary.

Sincerely,
A troubled seminarian

Since this broken young man had not identified himself publicly. I read and discussed his letter with the student body the following morning. Many of the three hundred young men who were present seemed moved by his words; for some, it undoubtedly reflected their own predicament as well. Following my lecture that morning, the 'troubled seminarian' came and introduced himself to me. He stood with tears streaming down his cheeks as he spoke of the great sense of inadequacy he had experienced since early childhood. Later, an administrator of the seminary told me that this young man was the last member of the student body whom he would have expected to feel this way. As I have observed so many times, this sense of inferiority is the best-kept secret of the year. It is harboured deep inside, where it can gnaw on the soul.

Sitting in the audience that same day was another student with the same kind of problems. However, he did not write me a letter. He never identified himself in any way. But three weeks after I left, he hanged himself in the basement of his apartment. One of the four men with whom he lived called long distance to inform me of the tragedy. He stated, deeply shaken, that the dead student's room-mates were so unaware of his problems that he hanged there five days before he was missed!

Not only do laymen fail to understand each other. It has been discouraging for me to see how often my professional colleagues (psychiatrists, psychologists, and counsellors) have overlooked inferiority as a most obvious root cause for emotional distress. Lack of self-esteem produces more symptoms of psychiatric disorders than any other factor yet identified.

Time and time again in my casework as a psychologist, I sit talking to a person with deep longings to be respected and accepted. How badly he needs human affection and kindness, as well as emotional support and suggestions for change. Yet if that same needy patient had gone to Dr. Sigmund Freud in his day, the immortal grandfather of psychoanalysis would have sat back in detached professionalism, analysing the patient's sexual repressions. If the patient had sought treatment from Dr. Arthur Janov, the innovator of primal therapy, he would have been encouraged to roll on the floor and scream like a baby. (How foolish that form of 'therapy' appears from my perspective!) Other modern therapists would have required the same patient to assault, and be assaulted by, other members of an 'encounter group', or remove his clothing in a group, or beat his mother and father with a belt. Believe it or not, one of the major areas of controversy at earlier psychiatric conferences involved the wisdom of female patients having sexual intercourse with their male therapists! Have we gone completely mad? Whenever men abandon their ethics they cease to make sense, regardless of their professional degrees and licences. Perhaps this is why psychiatry is called 'the study of the id by the odd.' (No disparagement is intended to the more orthodox profession of psychiatry, itself.)

The most successful approach to therapy for a broken patient, I firmly believe, is to convey the following message with conviction (though perhaps not with words): 'Life has been tough and you've had your share of suffering. To this point, you've faced your problems without much human support and there have been times when your despair has been overwhelming. Let me, now, share that burden. From this moment forward, I am interested in you as a person; you deserve and shall have my respect. As best as possible, I want you to quit worrying about your troubles. Instead, confide them to me. Our concentration will be on the present and the future, and together we will seek appropriate solutions.'

Suddenly, the beleaguered patient no longer feels alone – the most depressing of human experiences. 'Someone cares! Someone understands! Someone assures me with professional confidence that he is certain I will survive. I'm not going to drown in this sea of despondency, as I feared. I have been thrown a life preserver by a friend who promises not to abandon me in the storm.' This is real therapy, and it exemplifies the essence of the Christian commandment that we 'bear one another's burdens.'

This same Christian principle offers the most promising solution to *your* inferiority and inadequacy, as well. I have repeatedly observed that a person's own needs and problems seem less threatening when he is busy helping someone else handle theirs! It is difficult to wallow in your own troubles when you are actively shouldering another person's load and seeking solutions to his problems. For each discouraged reader who feels unloved and shortchanged by life, I would recommend that you consciously make a practice of giving to others. Visit the sick. Bake something for your neighbours. Use your car for those without transportation. And perhaps most importantly, learn to be a good listener. The world is filled with lonely, disheartened people like yourself, and you are in an excellent position to empathise with them. And while you're doing it, I guarantee that your own sense of uselessness will begin to fade.

For those of you who have struggled with inferiority throughout your lives, isn't it about time you made friends with yourself? Aren't there enough headaches in life without beating your skull against that old brick wall of inadequacy, year after year? If I were to draw a caricature that would symbolise the millions of adults with low self-esteem, I would depict a bowed, weary traveller. Over his shoulder I would place the end of a mile-long chain to which is attached tons of scrap iron, old tyres, and garbage of all types. Each piece of junk is inscribed with the details of some humiliation – a failure – an embarrassment – a rejection from the past. He could let go of the chain and free himself from that heavy load which immobilises and exhausts him, but he is somehow convinced that it must be dragged throughout life. Like the troubled seminarian, he is paralysed by its weight. So he plods onward, digging a furrow in the good earth as he goes.

You can free yourself from the weight of the chain if you will but turn it loose. Your inferiority is based on a distortion of reality seen through childish eyes. The standards by which you have assessed yourself are themselves changing and fickle. Dr. Maxwell Maltz, the plastic surgeon who authored *Psycho-Cybernetics*, said women came to him in the 1920s requesting that their breasts be reduced in size. Today they are asking that he pump them up with silicone. False values! In King Solomon's biblical love song, he asked his bride to overlook his dark skin that had occurred from exposure to the sun. In his day, right meant white. But now the brown brother Solomon would be the pride of the beach. False values! Modern women are ashamed to admit that they carry an extra ten pounds of weight, yet Rembrandt would have loved to paint their plump, rotund bodies. False values! Don't you see that your personal worth is not really dependent on the opinions of others and the temporal, fluctuating values they represent? The sooner you can accept the transcending worth of your humanness, the sooner you can come to terms with yourself. I must agree with the writer who said: 'While in the race to save our face, why not conquer inner space?' It's not a bad idea.

Questions and Answers

(1) *I am depressed much of the time and worry about whether or not my kids will be affected by my moods. Are children typically sensitive to parental discouragement and depression?*

According to Dr. Norman S. Brandes, child psychiatrist, children are very sensitive to depression in the adults around them. They often become depressed themselves, even though adults think they've hidden their despair from the children. Furthermore, you are being watched carefully by your children and they are 'learning' how you deal with frustration. In short, you are effectively teaching them, through your own depression, to react similarly in the future.

If your depression continues to be chronic, as you indicated, I would suggest that you seek professional advice. Begin with your physician, who may recognise a physical cause for your constant discouragement. If not, he may refer you for psychological assistance. This does not mean you are mentally ill or neurotic. It may indicate nothing more than that you need to examine the things that are bothering you with the help of a competent counsellor.

(2) *When the women you surveyed indicated 'low self-esteem' as their most common source of depression, did physical attractiveness play a role in their feelings? Don't they get over that sensitivity in adulthood?*

There were many factors involved in the poor self-concepts of the women surveyed. Many of them reported a lack of romantic affection and appreciation from their husbands, which made them feel unneeded and unloved. Others felt isolated and unfulfilled in their roles as wives and mothers (which is, I believe, one of the most important jobs in the world. The stability of a nation actually depends on how well women handle this family responsibility! Nevertheless, women have been told repeatedly that child rearing is somehow unworthy of their time, and those who are cast in this mould often feel trapped and unnecessary).

Beyond the reasons cited above, physical attractiveness did have a dominant role to play in the inadequacy indicated on the questionnaire. The necessity for beauty does not end in adolescence. It continues to determine human worth to some degree until late in life. Let me give you an example of what I mean. I counselled a young woman who had been a beautiful airline stewardess a few years earlier. She was happily married to a man who was proud of her beauty. Then a most unfortunate thing happened. She was in a tragic automobile accident which scarred her face and twisted her body. Her back was broken and she was destined to walk with a cane for the rest of her life. She was no longer attractive and her husband quickly lost interest in her sexually. Their divorce followed shortly. As a cripple she could no longer serve as a stewardess, of course, and she found it difficult to obtain a job of any type. In this instance, a girl with high personal worth plunged to a position of little social status in one brief moment. Her true value as a human being should not have been affected by her accident, but it certainly was.

While there are many causes for low self-esteem among women today, that old nemesis called 'the uglies' (which every woman experiences at least occasionally) keeps doing it dirty work throughout our society. As indicated, it isn't the only source of depression, but it remains a major one.

AFTERTHOUGHT: If you doubt the influence of physical attractiveness in your own value system, you may want to give yourself the supreme test. Go into an exclusive clothing store, where all the salespeople are beautifully tailored and combed. Then walk up to a four-way mirror and examine yourself from all angles. Scrutinise the back of your head, your profile, and your rear end. If you're 'normal', this experience will destroy you for at least three days!

5

COPING CAN BE CATCHING

We must now, in the concluding pages of this diatribe, turn
our attention to the meaning of behaviour, itself. Have you
ever wondered how two children raised in the same home can
be so unique and individualistic? How can one child be
reverently quiet and withdrawn, while another, produced
and raised by the same parents, is noisy and self-assertive?
Extending the questions further, what determines the
various personality patterns of human beings? Why is one
man kind and gentle while another is mean and hateful?
What are the ingredients from which such lifelong personality characteristics are constructed in a young child? These
questions could represent the most important subject matter
in this book, and their answers may be the most useful. Why?
Because the art of good parenthood begins with the fundamental skill of being able to get behind the eyes of the child,
seeing what he sees, feeling what he feels, hoping what he
hopes. It is this awareness of his world that permits a parent
(or teacher or grandparent) to hold the child when he is
threatened, or love him when he is lonely, or teach him when
he is inquisitive, or discipline him when he knows he is
wrong. The success of the entire parent-child relationship
depends on this perceptive skill. How often do teenagers
complain, 'My parents don't understand me!' They are pro-
nouncing judgment on their parents' inability to 'mind read'
as I've described. But how can this ability be attained? It is
acquired by developing an understanding of the meaning of

behaviour, and the chapter which follows is devoted to that objective.

A portion of the human temperament is apparently pre-determined by heredity, although the real heavyweight in shaping the personality is that some old companion, *inferiority*. You see, damage to the ego (loss of self-worth) actually equals or exceeds the pain of physical discomfort in intensity. In fact, I have seen people experiencing extreme physical pain, and I have witnessed others whose self-esteem had completely crumbled. I believe the latter is worse! It gnaws on the soul through the conscious mind by day and in the dreams by night. So painful is its effect that our entire emotional apparatus is designed to protect us from its oppression. *In other words, a sizable proportion of all human activity is devoted to the task of shielding us from the inner pain of inferiority.* I believe this to be *the* most dominant force in life, even exceeding the power of sex in its influence. Therefore, if we are to understand the meaning of behaviour in our boys and girls, husband or wife, friends and neighbours – and even our enemies – then we must begin by investigating the ways human beings typically cope with self-doubts and personal inadequacies.

The remainder of this chapter is devoted to the six most common ways children (and adults) cope with inferiority. I don't want to overstate my case, but I believe these six personality patterns offer the most direct and accurate explanation of human behaviour that I have seen. Most children adopt one or more of these avenues of defence. Each parent is encouraged to look within the following pages for the footprints of his own child, and while doing so, he might even find the sand-filled remnants of his own tracks.

Pattern No. 1

I'LL WITHDRAW

One of the most common ways of dealing with inadequacy and inferiority is to surrender, completely and totally. The individual who chooses this approach has concluded in his own mind that he *is* inferior. He measures his worth according to the attributes we have discussed (and others), making this reluctant admission to himself:

Yes it's true! I am a failure, just as I feared. Even now people are laughing at me. Where can I hide?

Having accepted his own unworthiness, which was his first mistake, he is forced to guard his wounded ego from further damage. Thus, 'caution' becomes his watchword. He withdraws into a shell of silence and loneliness, choosing to take no chances nor assume any unnecessary emotional risks. He would never initiate a conversation, nor speak in a group, nor enter a contest, nor ask for a date, nor run for election, nor even defend his honour when it is trampled. From the early years on through life, he copes with inferiority by projecting a defensive meekness, having learned that the best way to save his face is to button his lip. As the comedian Jackie Vernon once said, 'The meek shall inherit the earth, because they'll be too timid to refuse it.'

Every school classroom is populated by several children who have admitted defeat to themselves. In the elementary grades they sit year after year in silence with eyes cast downward. Their peers know them as 'shy' or 'quiet', but seldom understand their true feelings. The withdrawing child is usually misjudged in two major ways: (1) Since he is quiet, reserved, and unresponsive, he is frequently assumed to be stuck-up and snobbish. Imagine that! The child (and adult) who is most overwhelmed with his own inferiority is blamed for thinking too highly of himself. How little we understand each other! (2) Because the withdrawing individual seldom speaks, it is assumed that he isn't thinking. Quite the opposite, his mind whirls with thoughts and feelings just like yours and mine. But he learns very early in life that the safest defence is to keep his mouth shut. (This system often backfires for a boy, however, since he becomes the unprotected target of the local bully.)

I believe we have much greater reason to be concerned

about the withdrawing child, from a psychological point of view, than the more aggressive troublemaker. Children at both extremes often need adult intervention; but the surrenderer is much less likely to get it. He doesn't bug anybody. He cooperates with his teacher and tries to avoid conflict with his peers. But his quiet manner is dangerously misleading. The adults in his life may fail to notice that his destructive self-image is rapidly solidifying and will never be pliable again. Considering all the alternative ways to cope with inferiority, withdrawal is probably the least effective and most painful. It is, in reality, no defence at all. The introspective adults who choose this approach are in a high-risk group for ulcers, migraine headaches, acute colitis, and other psychosomatic illnesses. Their caution prevents them from releasing the emotional tension trapped within, often resulting in a physical blowout somewhere inside. As housewives, they pull within the walls of their homes, biting their nails, peeking out at the world going by, often weeping in loneliness. They live with depression, and too frequently their only ally is a bottle of booze, leading them down the road to secret alcoholism. A husband with the same response to his problems may become a henpecked nonentity. Since he lacks the ego strength to lead the family, he must be content to follow in silence. All in all, withdrawing (in its extreme sense) is not a very successful approach to the problem of inferiority.

Pattern No. 2

I'LL FIGHT

The *identical* feelings which motivate one child to withdraw from society will urge a more aggressive boy or girl to fight in response. Instead of surrendering to inferiority, like the withdrawing child, the fighter is angered by what he sees. He carries a chip on his shoulder and dares anyone to knock it off. He looks for any excuse to lash out and his temper can be triggered by the most insignificant provocation. If he is tough enough to back up his threats, he may become the terror of the playground. Later in life, he develops into a mean, temperamental old malcontent, always looking for a hassle with somebody – anybody. (My deepest sympathy is with the person who is married to a confirmed fighter!)

Although inferiority is always discomforting, the fighter is less vulnerable to its impact than a withdrawing child. At least he has a defence, even if it is an antisocial one. The realisation of this fact creates the climate for a dramatic personality reversal during the early teen years. Not infrequently, a quiet, timid child will creep into adolescence as a cautious surrenderer. He has avoided conflict all through his life and has suffered accordingly. Then during the natural antagonism of adolescence, he learns almost by accident that it hurts less to fight than withdraw. And suddenly, this shy, meek youngster will become a hostile, aggressive fighter. His parents shake their heads in disbelief as their cooperative teenager declares total war on everyone in sight.

When the intensity of inferiority is greatest, the shift from withdrawing to fighting may involve violence and viciousness. I would recall to your attention the details of Lee Harvey Oswald's life. He attempted to cope with his problems in numerous ways, but he was blocked at every turn. Running away to Russia (withdrawal) did not help, nor was his predicament eased by submission to his wife (surrender). He was unsuccessful in all of his less aggressive attempts at coping. Finally, as it often does, his grief turned to anger. Please underscore this point: *a sudden outburst of aggressive behaviour is likely to occur any time a more passive approach has consistently failed to ease the severe pain of inferioirity.*

I have also been studying the childhood of the other convicted Kennedy assassin, Sirhan Sirhan. The background of the sad young man (who attended my church for a time) is remarkably similar in emotional tone to that of Oswald. According to Paul O'Neil's account reported in *Life* magazine (June 21, 1968), Sirhan was 'unstable and unhappy' throughout childhood. When his family first came to America, he was bothered by his own strangeness as a foreigner in the eyes of his classmates. Sirhan's father,

Bishara, 'beat his children with sticks and fists when they disobeyed him and once held a hot iron to one of Sirhan's heels.' Like Oswald, he was small in stature and never associated with girls through his entire school career.

It seems apparent that Sirhan's method of dealing with inferiority was to withdraw and surrender. Quoting *Life* magazine further, 'He was polite. He was quiet. He concentrated hard on his studies as a schoolboy and on an obscure religious philosophy as an adult.' Furthermore, he 'kept out of trouble, blended as if he were transparent, into the student body of Pasadena's John Muir High School.' This lad who was destined to become a calculating assassin was, of all things, a shy and unassuming student.

After high-school graduation, young Sirhan began a desperate search for adequacy – which was no more successful than had been the quest of Lee Harvey Oswald. Because of his very short stature, he had a burning desire to race thoroughbred horses. Becoming a successful jockey offered the brightest hope for achieving self-respect, and he invested every ounce of energy in pursuit of that dream. He applied for a job at Santa Anita Race Track in Arcadia, but the officials there saw quickly that he lacked the reflexes and experience to handle the temperamental animals. Instead, he was given a job as a 'hot walker' and exercise boy, the least respectable job on the track. (A 'hot walker' leads the horses around the track after they have been running.) Even more humiliating was the fact that Sirhan frequently fell off his mount, earning him the title of 'real-estate buyer' in the jargon of the horsemen. Finally, he was severely thrown from a filly and was taken to a nearby hospital, where the attendants found him furious. His humiliation was complete, and he raged at everyone who tried to treat him. Sirhan gave up horses that day; he had failed to reach his most cherished dream. He hadn't even come close.

Shortly thereafter he suffered the crowning blow. Sirhan identified himself completely with the Arab cause in the Six Day War against Israel. Thus, the crushing Arab defeat became his personal loss, agitating him beyond containment. At this point, perhaps before, the 'quiet', 'polite', young man who 'kept out of trouble' became a fighter. The rest of the story is history.

In summary, both Kennedy assassins, Oswald and Sirhan, appear to have followed the same well-trodden pathway: (1) they experienced deep-seated feelings of inferiority; (2) they sought to cope by withdrawal and surrender: (3) their vain attempts to achieve adequacy were miserable failures; and (4) they exploded in violence. This pattern fits Dr. Karl Menninger's description of a typical assassin, cited in Albert Rosenfeld's article 'The Psychobiology of Violence' in the issue of *Life* mentioned above: 'An anonymous, faceless, embittered man who feels self-important and ambitious. He also feels unloved, lonely and alienated. He wants desperately to be somebody but never makes it. . . .' Dr. Menninger was certainly on target with regard to Oswald and Sirhan. These two extremes were reported here to illustrate the dramatic shift from a passive coping behaviour pattern to a more violent one.

The movement from withdrawal to aggression can be seen in other less deadly instances throughout our society. In my opinion, this principle is behind the tremendous hostility which fuels the Women's Liberation movement. Several decades ago, our society foolishly began to devalue the importance of being a wife and mother. American women were made to feel unneeded and unnecessary – and even foolish – in this homemaking role. 'I'm just a housewife,' they were taught to say. The burning message of inferiority was preached by the media and even through the attitudes of husbands, yet the responsibilities of children and the home made it impossible for women to escape. Suddenly, the sense of unworthiness initiated an emotion-charged reversal from acceptance to aggression. It is most unfortunate that wives and mothers were not given the status and respect that their position deserves, precipitating the angry movement which now threatens to undermine the American family.

In summary, fighting is a second important way of dealing with inferiority, accounting for a certain proportion of the violence that now permeates our society. It produces much of the antagonism of adolescence, and is likely to appear whenever less aggressive personality patterns fail to reduce the pain of inferiority.

Pattern No. 3
I'LL BE A CLOWN

Another very common way to deal with inferiority is to laugh it off. By making an enormous joke out of everything, the clown conceals the self-doubt that churns inside. Phyllis Diller, the frazzle-haired comedienne, has made a fortune by laughing at her physical disaster! She said she had the first peek-a-boo dress – first people would peek, and then they'd boo! (Incidentally, it would be a mistake to think Miss Diller does not care about her looks. By her own account, she was a shy, inadequate, withdrawing individual during her younger days, constantly aware of her unattractiveness. Then suddenly, she discovered a less painful – and more lucrative – way of coping: through self-effacing laughter. The role she now plays on stage certainly does not represent her true feelings, as revealed by the face-lifting she underwent a few years ago. 'I had begun to look pretty horrible. Not funny-horrible – just bad,' she explained.)

Being a clown is a particularly useful approach for the individual with a very obvious facial flaw. How would you deal, for example, with Jimmy Durante's nose if it were stuck on the edge of your face? Everywhere you went, people would look at it and laugh. All through childhood you would be hounded about that 'pound of flesh' out in front. What could you do, stay furious at the whole world? Would you beat up everyone who snickered at it? Your best bet would be to learn to laugh about it. Accordingly, most comedians get their 'training' during childhood, when being a clown presents itself as a useful response to inferiority. Jonathan Winters admits his humour is a defence against childhood hurts. His parents were divorced when he was seven, and he used to cry when alone because other children said he had no father. Winters now recognises the wisdom of Thackeray's observation that 'Humour is the mistress of tears.'

Not only did inferiority play a key role in the training of many comedians, this subject continues to provide their favourite source of humorous material. Rodney Dangerfield, for example, has based his entire act on the line, 'I don't get no respect!' Joan Rivers jokes incessantly about her ugliness as a girl. She said she was such a 'dog' that her father had to throw a bone down the aisle to get her married. But in my opinion, the comedian who makes the most effective use of inferiority is the scrawny introvert, Woody Allen. The following story from Woody's childhood comes alive when he tells it:

Woody was on his way to his violin lesson when he passed the pool hall where 'Floyd' and his friends hung out. They were stealing hubcaps (from moving cars). Floyd called Woody an insulting name as he passed, and being a 'cocky kid', Woody announced that he didn't take that from anybody! He put down his violin and said, 'If you want to address me, you will call me Master Haywood Allen!' Woody said he spent that winter in a wheelchair. A team of doctors laboured to remove a violin from his skull. His only good fortune was that it wasn't a cello.

Hasn't every boy in the world been tyrannised by 'Floyd' sometime during his childhood? He was certainly well represented in my hometown.

Every schoolteacher is well acquainted with the clowns in her classroom. The Board of Education assigns at least one per class to make sure that she earns each dollar of her salary. These skilled disruptors are usually boys, often have reading or other academic problems, may be small in stature, and will do anything for a laugh (eat worms, risk expulsion from school, hang by one toe from a tree, etc.) Their parents are usually unappreciative of the humour, and may never recognise that the clown, the fighter, and the surrenderer all have one important thing in common: inferiority.

Pattern No. 4

I'll Deny Reality

I worked with the teacher of Jeff, a seven-year-old child who wore heavy leather gloves to school every day. He was rarely seen without his gloves, even on the warmest days. His teacher insisted that he remove them when in the classroom because he could scarcely hold a pencil with the thickly padded fingers. But the moment Jeff was sent to recess or lunch, the gloves made their reappearance. Jeff's teacher could not understand the motive for this behaviour; all through the school year he never wavered in his desire to wear those hot, cumbersome gloves. In discussing the matter with me, she casually mentioned that this boy was the only black child in a room full of white children. His feelings were seemingly obvious at that point. When wearing a long-sleeve shirt or coat, the only black skin Jeff could see was on his hands. By wearing the gloves, he hid the feature which marked him as different from every other child in his room.

Jeff was, in effect, denying reality. He refused to see or think about the source of his inadequacy. His approach is one of the favourite coping behaviours in our society, today. It is primarily responsible for the enormous problem of alcoholism in this country! There are more than 9 million *known* alcoholics in America, today. One out of every four citizens is a close family member of a confirmed alcoholic. What better example of emotional escape can there be than living in a drunken stupor most of the time?

There are other convenient ways to deny reality for a short trip. Undoubtedly, this need for temporary escape plays a key role in the drug-abuse phenomenon that has swept through the younger generation. Massive self-doubt simply can't be ignored. It must be handled in some manner, and for the young, the most direct resolution comes in the form of a capsule or syringe. My work with life-long addicts in the Federal Narcotics Symposium, Los Angeles, confirmed my suspicion of the part played by inferiority in their dependence on drugs.

There is one other convenient way to deny painful reality: through psychotic experience. The psychotic individual merely pulls down a mental shade and creates his own dream world. (Psychosis has other causes, as well, involving emotional and/or biochemical difficulties.) He 'copes' with his problems by refusing to believe they are there. This experience, inappropriately called mental illness, is the most unfortunate alternative available for adoption.

Do you, the reader, now understand the point I made in the first chapter, repeated below?

> Thus, whenever the keys to self-esteem are seemingly out of reach for a large percentage of the people, as in twentieth-century America, then widespread 'mental illness', neuroticism, hatred, alcoholism, drug abuse, violence, and social disorder will certainly occur. Personal worth is not something human beings are free to take or leave. We must have it, and when it is un-attainable, everybody suffers.

Many of the seemingly unsolvable social problems we are now facing represent desperate but unsuccessful attempts to cope with inferiority. When the incidence of self-doubt is greatest, accompanied by the unavailability of acceptable solutions, then the probability of irresistible social disorder is maximised. Call it Dobson's Law, if you wish. Whatever you call it, we are witnessing the phenomenon today.

Pattern No. 5

I'LL CONFORM

One of the great American myths is that we are a nation of rugged individualists. We really have ourselves fooled at this point. We like to think of ourselves as Abraham Lincolns, Patrick Henrys, and cowboys, standing tall and courageous in the face of social rejection. But that image is palpably uncharacteristic of most of us. In truth, we are a nation of social cowards. It seems to me that a major proportion of our energy is expended in trying to be like everyone else, cringing in fear of true individuality. Dean Martin once said, 'Show me a man who doesn't know the meaning of the word *fear*, and I'll show you a dummy who gets beat up a lot!' In our case however, we are not afraid of being beat up; it is ridicule and rejection that motivate our concern.

Conformity, then, presents itself as the fifth personality pattern in response to inferiority. Those who adopt it may be social doormats, afraid to express their own opinions. They seek to be liked by everyone, regardless of the expense to their own convictions and beliefs. For adolescents, whom I've already described, the urge to conform dictates most of their activity for a period of ten or more years. Accordingly, adolescent behaviour is the most contagious phenomenon shared from one human being to another. Last year, for example, a teenage choir was singing the 'Battle Hymn of the Republic' in a live performance. During a high point in the emotional presentation, one youngster near the front row fainted and crumpled to the floor. The director went on with his performance, but the suggestion of fainting had been planted in fifty-two impressionable heads. Boom! The second singer went down. Boom! Boom! Two more hit the deck. The mania spread like wildfire. Five more vocalists blanched, buckled, and disappeared from the back row. When the director reached the last 'Glory, Glory Halle-lujah!' twenty members of his choir were out cold on the floor. That, folks, is conformity at its best.

Conformity also combines with denial of reality in inspiring the drug-abuse problem among the young. For this reason, I'm sorry to say, narcotics usage among teenagers will not be conquered by better education regarding its hazards. The kids already know the consequences of drug usage – probably better than we do. They are not deaf, and their use of narcotics is usually done in spite of the obvious price tag. Though we have to support our educational efforts with the young (it is our only hope for change), the drug problem will continue until it is no longer fashionable to 'trip out'. When it becomes disgraceful to use drugs, the epidemic will be over – but not a minute sooner.

Conformity plays such a key role in our social life that an entire book could be written on this subject, alone. Suffice to say at this point, however, that it offers a readily available response to inadequacy and low self-esteem.

Pattern No. 6

I'LL COMPENSATE

I have presented five approaches to inferiority which comprise the most common personality patterns today. The selection of a particular pattern, however, may not be a matter of personal choice. It has always been surprising for me to observe how rigidly society dictates which of the five approaches an individual is expected to pursue. Everyone knows, for example, that the fat person is supposed to be a jolly clown. It would seem strange to see him fight or withdraw, because we've come to expect smiles on the faces of our pudgy friends. On the other hand, a redhead is told of his 'hot temper' from his early days and is expected to be a fighter. A girl with a weak chin and soft voice is moulded into the withdrawing pattern, whether she likes it or not. A teenager is required to conform, fight, and perhaps deny reality (in fact, adolescents can play all five roles in confusing array because their personalities are in a state of re-evaluation and change). This dramatic social force, then, stamps its indelible image on our psyche and surprisingly, we do what we're told!

Someone has said:

> We are not what we think we are . . .
> We are not even what *others* think we are . . .
> We are what we *think* others think we are.

There is great truth in this statement. Each of us evaluates what we believe other people are thinking about us, and then we often play that prescribed role. This explains why we wear a very different 'face' with different groups. A doctor may be an unsmiling professional with his patients, being reserved and wise in their presence. They 'see' him that way and he complies. That evening, however, he is reunited with his former college friends who remember him as a post-adolescent screwball. His personality may oscillate 180 degrees between afternoon and night, being totally un-recognisable if seen by an amazed patient. Similarly, most of us *are* what we think others think we are. This makes in-feriority more difficult to treat because we not only must change a person's self-concept, but also his concept of what everyone else thinks, too. The double aspects of that assign-ment are often overlooked by therapists.

Now we come to the final point. The five personality patterns described in the preceding pages are more or less maladaptive. They offer momentary methods of coping with inferiority, but the self-doubt lingers. There is a better alter-native, and it was described earlier as compensation. The unconscious reasoning of a compensater goes like this:

I refuse to be drowned in a sea of inferiority. I can achieve adequacy through success if I work hard at it. Therefore, I will pour all my energy into basketball (or painting, or sewing, or politics, or graduate school, or gardening, or motherhood, or salesmanship, or Wall Street – or for a child, elementary school, or piano playing, or baton-twirling or football).

This kind of compensation provides the emotional energy for virtually every kind of successful human behaviour, as described earlier. In a famous study by Victor and Mildred Goertzel, entitled *Cradles of Eminence*, the home backgrounds of four hundred highly successful people were investigated. These four hundred subjects were individuals who had made it to the top. They were men and women whose names you would recognise as brilliant or outstanding in their respec-tive fields (Churchill, Gandhi, F. D. Roosevelt, Schweitzer,

Einstein, Freud, etc.). The intensive investigation into their early home lives yielded some surprising findings:

(1) Three-fourths of the children [were] troubled – by poverty: by a broken home; by rejecting, over-possessive, estranged, or dominating parents; by financial ups and downs; by physical handicaps; or by parental dissatisfaction over the children's school failures or vocational choices.

(2) Seventy-four of eighty-five writers of fiction or drama and sixteen of twenty poets [came] from homes where, as children, they saw tense psychological dramas played out by their parents.

(3) Handicaps such as blindness; deafness; being crippled, sickly, homely, undersized, or overweight; or having a speech defect [occurred] in the childhoods of over one-fourth of the sample.

It seems very apparent that the need to compensate for their disadvantages was a major factor in their struggle for personal achievement. It may even have been *the* determining factor.

There have been thousands, perhaps millions, of inadequate persons who used compensation to achieve esteem and confidence. Perhaps the most classic illustration is seen in the life of Eleanor Roosevelt, the former First Lady. Being orphaned at ten, she underwent a childhood of utter anguish. She was very homely and never felt she really belonged to anybody. According to Victor Wilson, Newhouse News Service, 'She was a rather humourless introvert, a young woman unbelievably shy, unable to overcome her personal insecurity and with a conviction of her own inadequacy.' The world knows, however, that Mrs. Roosevelt did rise above her emotional shackles. As Wilson said, '. . . from some inner wellspring, Mrs. Roosevelt summoned a tough, unyielding courage, tempered by remarkable self-control and self--discipline. . . .' That 'inner wellspring' has another appropriate name: compensation!

Obviously, one's *attitude* towards a handicap determines its impact on his life. It has become popular to blame adverse circumstances for irresponsible behaviour; i.e., poverty *causes* crime, broken homes *produce* juvenile delinquents, a sick society imposes drug addiction on its youth. This fallacious reasoning removes all responsibility from the shoulders of the individual. The excuse is hollow. We must each decide what we will do with inner inferiority or outer hardship.

Admittedly, it requires courage to triumph despite unfavourable odds. Compensation takes guts, for some much more than others. The easier path is to wallow in self-pity – to freak-out on drugs – to hate the world – to run – to withdraw – to compromise. Regardless of the ultimate course of action, however, the choice is ours alone and no one can remove it from us. Hardship does not *determine* our behaviour, but it clearly influences it.

As I have already discussed in Strategy No. 4, parents can open the door to responsible 'choices' by giving their children the means by which to compensate, beginning during their middle childhood years. If they do not accomplish that vital parental task, they increase the probability that their children will adopt one of the other less successful patterns of behaviour. Of the six alternatives, compensating is by far the best bet for *your* child.

Questions and Answers

(1) *I'm interested in your statement that angry, hostile behaviour is most often a response to inferiority. Can you give some other examples of this motivating force?*

That is an easy question to answer. In fact, anger has become *the* accepted way of dealing with feelings of inferiority today. In addition to the Women's Liberation movement, which I've mentioned, prolonged inferiority powers the angry black civil rights movement ('Black is Beautiful'), as well as the Gay Liberation movement, the Chicano movement (Brown Berets), and the Jewish Defence League, among others. Inferiority even motivates wars and international politics. What did Hitler tell the German people in 1939? He assured them that their loss in World War I was the fault of their leaders; they were really *superior* human beings. He was capitalising on their inferiority as a defeated, humiliated people. I suspect that their willingness to fight was more motivated by this new pride than any other factor. More recently, the 1973 Arab attack on Israel was primarily intended to avenge their disgraceful loss in the Six Day War of 1967. The world scoffed at the Arab impotence, which was more intolerable than the loss of land or the death and destruction they sustained. One Arab journalist was quoted in *Time* magazine (Octover 22, 1973) shortly after the 1973 war began:

It doesn't matter if the Israelis eventually counterattack and drive us back. What matters is that the world now no longer will laugh at us.

Recent evidence even suggests that inferiority is the major force behind the rampaging incidence of rape today. If sexual intercourse was the only objective of a rapist, then he could find satisfaction with a prostitute. But something else is involved. Most rapists apparently want to humiliate their victims. Having been unsuccessful with girls through adolescence and young adulthood, they seek sexual superiority by disgracing and exploiting defenceless women.

How about aggressive violence in American classrooms, which has been increasing steadily in recent years? Can it be attributed to the frustration of inferiority? I'm inclined to believe so. And what better explanation can there be for the vandalism which destroys millions of dollars worth of school property each year? The educators impose inadequacy on the students by day and suffer their retaliation under the cover of night.

The examples are legion. That is why I have contended that social chaos in all its forms can be laid at the door of inadequacy and inferiority. There are numerous other causes, of course, but none so powerful.

(2) *You said a person acts according to the way he thinks he is seen. Can parents use this principle to train their children?*

Certainly. If you let a child know you think he is lazy, sloppy, untruthful, unpleasant, and thoughtless, he'll probably prove you are right. Obviously, it is better to make him stretch to reach a positive image than stoop to match one at ground level.

(3) *My son is only three and he's still extremely shy. He won't let anyone hold him but his own family, and he can't even look a stranger in the eye. How can I pull him out?*

At his age, shyness is nothing to worry about. He is retreating to the safety of the familiar because he is threatened by the new. That's a reasonable manoeuvre. It would be a mistake for you to tear him loose from the security of your arms too quickly, although you should begin to move in that direction. If this shyness and bashfulness continue unchecked through this next year, I would recommend that you utilise the time-honoured approach of nursery school to help with the task. It would be wise to introduce him gradually to a good preschool programme, accomplished in four distinct steps:

(1) Talk about the exciting things he will soon do in preschool. Try to whet his appetite during the two weeks prior to entry.
(2) Take him to visit the teacher at least twice, perhaps on consecutive days, when no other children are involved. Tip off the teacher as to the name of his dog or cat and other familiar topics they can discuss.
(3) Let him observe the other children in play from the sidelines with you standing nearby. No interaction with other children is required on this day.

(4) The fourth step brings 'plunge-in' day – even if he yells bloody murder when you leave. His peers will do the rest.

In short, shyness in a three-year-old is not unusual and does not warrant concern. If it does become necessary to pry him loose in the years that follow, it will better be accomplished by nudging rather than ripping his moorings.

(4) *Specifically, would you rather your own child 'withdraw' or 'fight'?*

That question is like asking if I would rather my child have the mumps or the measles. They are both diseases and I prefer neither. Extreme withdrawal and extreme aggression are both signs of emotional pressure. If forced to choose between these two patterns of behaviour, however, I would take the fighter. His discomfort is likely to be more manageable.

6

THE ONLY TRUE VALUES

Finally, we come back to the point where we began, with the question of social values. Having rejected physical attractiveness, intelligence, and materialism as determiners of human worth, we must now decide what will take their place. Have you consciously examined the values which you are teaching to your children? Are you following a well-conceived game plan on their behalf, instilling attitudes and concepts which are worthy of their dedication? The human spirit must have something meaningful in which to believe, and the instructional responsibility is much too important to handle in a haphazard manner.

I believe *the* most valuable contribution a parent can make to his child is to instil in him a genuine faith in God. What greater ego satisfaction could there be than knowing that the Creator of the Universe is acquainted with me, personally? That He values me more than the possessions of the entire world; that He understands my fears and my anxieties; that He reaches out to me in immeasurable love when no one else cares; that His only Son actually gave His life for me; that He can turn my liabilities into assets and my emptiness into fullness; that a better life follows this one, where the present handicaps and inadequacies will all be eliminated – where earthly pain and suffering will be no more than a dim memory! What a beautiful philosophy with which to 'clothe' your tender child. What a fantastic message of hope and encouragement for the broken teenager who has been crushed by life's circumstances. This is self-esteem at its richest, not dependent on the whims of birth or social judgment, or the cult of the superchild, but on divine decree. If this be the opiate of the people, as Karl Marx said, then I have staked my entire life on the validity of its promise!

Why do I stress the role of the Christian faith so strongly in reference to our children's self-esteem and worthiness? Because this belief offers the only way of life which can free us from the tyranny of the self. Make no mistake about it. The human ego is a cold-blooded dictator. When it is unsatisfied, as with Lee Harvey Oswald and so many of his contemporaries, it can paralyse its victim, destroying every vestige of confidence and initiative. When it is pampered, on the other hand, its thirst and greed merely become ever more unsatiable. Unlike the appetite for food, water, sex, and other physiological requirements of the body, the need for self-esteem becomes more demanding as it is gratified. The great military generals of the world, for example, being honoured and glorified by millions of soldiers and civilians, have not typically become more humble and self-effacing as they rose to power and fame. General Douglas MacArthur, General George Patton, Field Marshal B. L. Montgomery, General Charles De Gaulle and the other Allied military leaders of World War II were hardly overburdened with humility and self-sacrifice. Likewise, kings and queens and politicians and athletic champions and renowned physicians all tend to become more egocentric as their social status rises. In fact, it has been my observation that the more exalted a person becomes, the more 'entitled' he is to reveal his infantile demands.

The two bloodiest murderers of all times, Joseph Stalin and Adolf Hitler, became drunk with the gratification of their own egos. As Stalin's power increased in Russia, he demanded more and more subservience and worship from his followers. He scattered statues, pictures, and monuments of himself throughout the land and named countless streets, landmarks, and even cities in his honour. As his pride grew, so did his brutality. Anyone who challenged his opinion even on trivial matters was soon to disappear from the face of the earth. And in one of the most shocking examples of self-aggrandisement ever displayed, he murdered many of the townfolk in the locale of his childhood, so he could rewrite his personal history without leaving contradictory witnesses! Can you imagine bringing an elderly teacher before a prison firing squad for doing nothing more offensive than remembering his former student? It is said that Stalin executed between ten and thirty million people in cold blood, many of whom died for nothing more substantial than that Stalin's unbridled ego demanded their removal!

The record of Adolf Hitler is better known, but no less horrifying. There is ample reason to believe that his pitiless extermination of six million Jews resulted from his belief that their race contributed to his own inferiority complex. Truly, the ego of man is a frightening tyrant when it is given full reign.

Again, the principles of Christianity can free us from this egotistical tyranny. They place the spotlight on others rather than on ourselves, while granting human worth on a completely different scale of values than does society. Jesus Christ never said that the beautiful people have an inside track; He never granted special favours for intellectuals; He is not partial to the wealthy; He is unimpressed by blueblood family heritage. In fact, He expressed His disdain for these and other social values in the sixteenth chapter of Luke, verse 15 (KING JAMES VERSION):

For that which is highly esteemed among men is abomination in the sight of God.

In other words, God actually hates the things which we value most highly, because He sees the folly of our worshipping that which we can keep for such a brief time.

But what *does* God value? We cannot substitute His system for ours unless we know what He has personally ordained. Fortunately, the Bible provides the key to God's value system for mankind, and in my judgment, it is composed of six all-important principles. They are: (1) devotion to God;

(2) love for mankind; (3) respect for authority; (4) obedience to divine commandments: (5) self-discipline and self-control and (6) humbleness of spirit. These six concepts are from the hand of the Creator, Himself, and are absolutely valid and relevant for our lives. When applied, they encourage a child to *seek* out the opportunities in this world, rather than forcing him to *hide* in lonely isolation. *They lead not to neuroticism and despair, as do man's values, but to emotional and physical health.* Isn't this what is meant in Isaiah 54:13 (KJV), stating: 'All thy children shall be taught of the Lord, and great shall be the peace of thy children'?

The healthy self-concept which Christ taught, then, involves neither haughtiness and pride nor inferiority and worthlessness. It is one of humble reverence for God and every member of His human family. We are to see our fellowman as neither better nor worse than ourselves; rather, we are to love them *as* ourselves, and that prescription puts the entire matter of self-worth into its proper perspective.

Try it – you'll like it!

Epilogue

It has been five years since I wrote the book you have just finished reading. And in that half-decade, our fast-moving society has convulsed through many important changes and developments. Nevertheless, the theme of *How to Build Confidence in Your Child* remains as relevant today as when it was originally written. An 'epidemic of inferiority' still rages among the young (and haunts the mature). A quick comparison of then and now will give evidence of this personal unrest: incidence of alcoholism: *up*; incidence of divorce: *up*; incidence of child abuse: *up*; incidence of rape: *up*; incidence of arson: *up*; incidence of murder: *up*; incidence of teen suicide: *up*; incidence of spiritual poverty and loneliness and depression: *definitely up*.

When writing the original manuscript, I attempted to show how these examples of social chaos (and especially unprovoked violent crime) are linked to low self-esteem in most cases. We began with the personal agony of Lee Harvey Oswald, and how it led to assassination of John Fitzgerald Kennedy. Likewise, the inner turmoil of Sirhan Sirhan set the stage for a similar assault on the president's brother, Robert Kennedy. Since those stormy days, hundreds of other violent crimes have validated this connection between self-hatred and senseless killings.

Gary Mark Gilmore, for example, was executed in Utah for the murder of an unarmed motel clerk. He was quoted in *Time* magazine (November 29, 1976) shortly before his death, 'My soul is on fire and is screaming to vacate this ugly house.' That one sentence expresses a lifetime of personal disgust and despair. In an earlier *Newsweek* article, we are given a look at the motivation of Lynette 'Squeaky' Fromme, who attempted to assassinate then-President Gerald Ford. Note the feelings of inadequacy which permeate her story:

> One night in 1967, a puffy-faced scraggly-haired girl of 17 sat on a sidewalk in Venice, California. She had always thought she was ugly and unloved, and she was crying. 'A man walked up,' she later recalled, 'and said, "Your father kicked you out of the house" . . . He asked me to come with him. I said no . . . and he said he'd like me to come but couldn't make up my mind for me. No one had ever treated me like that – he didn't push me – so I picked up all I had and went with him. That was Charles Manson.' The girl was Lynette Alice Fromme, Squeaky to her friends, who last week stood on another California sidewalk and aimed a gun at Gerald Ford (*Newsweek*, September 15, 1975, page 18).

Later in the same article Squeaky explained why she was drawn to a man like Manson. 'A dog goes to somebody who loves it, and takes care of it,' she said. And speaking of a convicted killer Charles Manson, an article appearing in the *Indianapolis Star*, October 16, 1975, reported an interview with Agnes Mahoney, who was principal of the elementary school when Manson attended as a child. Several of her comments were especially relevant.

> At about this point in Manson's life, his mother was charged with adultery and left town to avoid facing trial, abandoning her son. Boys School records list Manson's father as 'unknown'. We tried to encourage Charles to participate in activities and sports, but he always had an excuse. He would say his arm hurt or he had a headache. *That's probably the most vivid thing I remember about him – the fact he was very shy and never mixed with other children . . .*

I remember once he told me that he felt no one liked him. I couldn't convince him otherwise (italics mine).

Miss Mahoney concluded, 'I still can't believe that shy little boy could turn into the man who did all those terrible things.'

Charles Manson's shy, introverted personality is characteristic of many other mass murderers, as well. Consider the bizarre example of David Berkowitz, the convicted 'Son of Sam' killer in New York City. He was captured after slaying six people and wounding seven more in 1976–77. His case was discussed by one psychologist from this point of view:

What could we learn from Son of Sam? Isolation is a bad thing. It ruins the psyche. One of the outstanding things here is the isolation of this man. Perhaps if he'd had someone to talk to his anger could have been drained off and he would not have killed. We cannot live without love.

Now obviously, not everyone who 'lives without love' becomes a mass murderer. My point is simply that social chaos of *all* varieties is rooted in feelings of worthlessness during the early years of childhood. And if that understanding is accurate, then the primary task of parents and teachers is made abundantly clear: We *must develop better methods of shielding young minds from the destructive forces that would crush or mutilate them*.

Towards that end, two additional strategies have become increasingly important in my approach to children during the past five years. In fact, the two suggestions that follow are now given more significance than the ten presented in the original text. Each of these strategies offers a fundamental preventative element which could be crucial in the life of a particularly vulnerable child. Perhaps you will find them useful.

Strategy No. 11
TEACH CHILDREN TO BE KIND

I was recently asked to respond to the question, 'What *one* feature should be changed in the Western culture in order to produce a higher percentage of emotionally healthy children and adults?' It is a stimulating question which would probably draw a unique answer from every professional who attempted a reply. But from my perspective, the most valuable revision would be for adults to begin actively teaching children to love and respect each other, (and, of course, to demonstrate that love in their own lives).

Far from manifesting kindness and sensitivity, however, children are often permitted to be terribly brutal and destructive, especially to the handicapped child, the ugly child, the slow-learning child, the uncoordinated child, the foreign child, the minority child, the small or the large child, and the child who is perceived to be different from his peers in even the most insignificant feature. And predictably, the damage inflicted on young victims often reverberates for a lifetime.

In counselling with neurotic patients, it is apparent that emotional problems usually originate in one of two places (or both): either from an unloving or unnourishing relationship with parents, or from an inability to gain acceptance and respect from peers. In other words, most emotional disorders (excepting organic illness) can be traced to destructive relationships with *people* during the first twenty years of life.

If this assumption is accurate, then adults should devote their creative energies to the teaching of *love* and *dignity*. And if necessary, we should *insist* that children approach each other with kindness. Can boys or girls be taught to respect their peers? They certainly can! Young people are naturally more sensitive and empathetic than adults. Their viciousness is a *learned* response, resulting from the highly competitive and hostile world which their leaders have permitted to develop. In short, children are destructive to the weak and lowly because we adults haven't bothered to teach them to 'feel' for one another.

Perhaps an example will help explain my concern. A woman told me recently about her experience as a room mother for her daughter's fourth-grade class. She visited the classroom on Valentine's Day to assist the teacher with the traditional party on that holiday. (As implied earlier, Valentine's Day can be the most painful day of the year for an unpopular child. Every student *counts* the number of valentines he is given as a direct measure of his social worth.) This mother said the teacher announced that the class was going to play a game which required the formation of boy-girl teams. That was her first mistake, since fourth graders have not yet experienced the happy hormones which draw the sexes together. The moment the teacher instructed the students to select a partner, all the boys immediately laughed and pointed at the homeliest and least-respected girl in the room. She was overweight, had protruding teeth, and was too withdrawn even to look anyone in the eye.

'Don't put us with Hazel,' they all said in mock terror. '*Anybody* but Hazel! She'll give us a disease! Ugh! Spare us from Horrible Hazel.' The mother waited for the teacher (a strong disciplinarian), to rush to the aid of the beleaguered little girl. But to her disappointment, nothing was said to the insulting boys. Instead, the teacher left Hazel to cope with that painful situation in solitude.

Ridicule by one's own sex is distressing, but rejection by the opposite sex is like taking a hatchet to the self-concept. What could this devastated child say in reply? How does an overweight fourth-grade girl defend herself against nine aggressive boys? What response could she make but to blush in mortification and slide foolishly into her chair? This child, whom God loves more than the possessions of the entire world, will never forget that moment, (or the teacher who abandoned her in this time of need).

If I had been the teacher of Hazel's class on that fateful Valentine's Day, those mocking, joking boys would have had a fight on their hands. Of course, it would have been better if the embarrassment could have been prevented by discussing the feelings of others from the first day of school. But if the conflict occurred as described, with Hazel's ego suddenly shredded for everyone to see, I would have thrown the full weight of my authority and respect on her side of the battle.

My spontaneous response would have carried this general theme: 'Wait just a minute! By what right do any of you boys say such mean, unkind things to Hazel? I want to know which of you is so perfect that the rest of us couldn't make fun of you in some way? I know you all very well. I know about your homes and your school records and some of your personal secrets. Would you like me to share them with the class, so we can all laugh at you the way you just did at Hazel? I could do it! I could make you want to crawl in a hole and disappear. But listen to me! You need not fear. I will *never* embarrass you in that way. Why not? Because it *hurts* to be laughed at by your friends. It hurts even more than a stubbed toe or a cut finger or a bee sting.'

'I want to ask those of you who were having such a good time a few minutes ago: Have you ever had a group of children make fun of you in the same way? If you haven't, then brace yourself. Some day it will happen to you, too. Eventually you will say something foolish . . . and they'll point at you and laugh in your face. And when it happens, I want you to remember what happened today.'

(*Then addressing the entire class*), 'Let's make sure that we learn something important from what took place here this afternoon. First, we *will not* be mean to each other in this class. We will laugh together when things are funny, but we will not do it by making one person feel badly. Second, I will *never* intentionally embarrass anyone in this class. You can count on that. Each of you is a child of God. He moulded you with His loving hands, and He has said that we all have equal worth as human beings. This means that Suzie is neither better nor worse than Charles or Mary or Brent. Sometimes I think maybe you believe a few of you are more important than others. It isn't true. Every one of you is priceless to God and each of you will live forever in eternity. That's how valuable you are. God loves every boy and girl in this room, and because of that, *I* love every one of you. He wants us to be kind to other people, and we're going to be practising that kindness through the rest of this year.'

When a strong, loving teacher comes to the aid of the least respected child in his class, as I've described, something dramatic occurs in the emotional climate of the room. Every child seems to utter an audible sigh of relief. The same thought is bouncing around in many little heads, 'If Hazel is safe from ridicule – even overweight Hazel – then I must be safe, too.' You see by defending the least popular child in the room, a teacher is demonstrating (1) that he has no 'pets'; (2) that he respects everyone; (3) that he will fight for anyone who is being treated unjustly. Those are three virtues which children value highly, and which contribute to mental health.

And may I suggest to parents, *defend the underdog in your neighbourhood*. Let it be known that you have the confidence to speak for the outcast. Explain this philosophy to your neighbours, and try to create an emotional harbour for the little children whose ship has been threatened by a storm of rejection. Don't be afraid to exercise *leadership* on behalf of a youngster who is being mauled. There is no more worthy investment of your time and energy.

This message is especially important for the children of Christians, who need to learn empathy and kindness during the early years. After all, Jesus gave the highest priority to the expression of love for God and for our neighbour, yet we often miss the emphasis in Christian education. For example, many Sunday schools diligently teach about Moses and Daniel and Joseph, but permit a chaotic situation to exist where their cavorting students are busily mutilating one another's egos. In fact, when a Sunday school lacks strong leadership as I've described, it can become the most 'dangerous' place in a child's week. That's why I like to see church workers spring to the defence of a harassed underdog, and in so doing, speak volumes about human worth and the love of Jesus.

But to be honest, I wonder why this suggestion is necessary. I find it difficult to comprehend why adults have to be encouraged to shield a vulnerable child whose defences have crumbled. What strange inhibition caused a loving teacher to stand immobile, while self-esteem was being assassinated in an overweight fourth-year girl? Why will car-pool drivers patently ignore brutal attacks that are hurled collectively at the least-popular rider? Why do mothers permit siblings to engage in emotional sabotage, with little more than a whimpered request for peace and quiet? Somehow, we adults feel we don't have a right to intervene in the antagonistic world of children. Well, it is my opinion that we *do* have the right; indeed, we have an obligation to say, 'Let it be understood that we *will not* treat one another with disrespect in this house! *Period*! And the deliberate violator of that rule will face certain unpleasant consequences!' That is one requirement which children will welcome, even while they are attempting to disobey it.

My views on this subject have been influenced significantly by watching the children of other cultures. Not every society is as competitive and threatening to young egos as ours. This fact was emphasised by a pediatrician friend who recently visited the People's Republic of China. To his surprise, Chinese children reacted very differently in a group situation than their American counterparts. They revealed almost none of the shyness, self-consciousness and reticence which is so characteristic of Western students when facing their peers. Despite the presence of American visitors in their classrooms, these children stood and recited their lessons without apparent anxiety. They participated in group demonstrations and dramas with unconcealed enthusiasm.

It would appear that the Chinese children are more confident because they do, in fact, live in a less-threatening environment. They are taught, as a product of the Communist system, to view their peers as 'comrades' and 'fellow workers'. Furthermore, competition between students is minimised and cooperation is stressed. The net effect is a less aggressive climate in which to grow.

If my earlier supposition is accurate (that early peer rejection is damaging to emotional health), then China's secure social climate should be correlated with a lower incidence of mental disorders in later adulthood. And predictably, that was the finding of Dr. Paul Lowinger, a psychiatrist who journeyed to China in 1975 to inspect that country's mental hospitals and attitudes towards emotional health. Quoted below are excerpts from his report published in *Medical Dimensions*, December 1976.

All across China, we dauntlessly questioned citizens about anxieties, marital problems, and family discord. We probed absenteeism from work, alienation, anti-social behaviour, and any other subjects we could think of that might cast some light on the general state of mental health in the People's Republic.

As we spoke with more and more people, it became evident that the Chinese were relatively free from psychoneurotic and personality disorders. In other words, there is very little depression, anxiety, fear, or alienation in China, especially when compared with Western society or with other emerging nations.

During the interviewing process. I was most interested in information concerning absenteeism from work, since I felt this indicated the kind of alienation that is often seen in personality disorders. In talking with people about this, we learned that it is virtually unknown for Chinese workers to be absent from their jobs unless they are physically ill and in treatment at a clinic or hospital. Of course, they told us, they do have vacations and take pregnancy leaves, but they go to work consistently and like their work. When I pressed him, however, one of our guides was finally able to recall someone he knew who had been discontented with his job and changed from hotel employment to factory work.

When we spoke to school administrators and teachers, we wanted to find out about the behavioural problems among young children and adolescents. The consensus was that behaviour problems are uncommon, although some children do learn more slowly than others. The teachers said it was rare for a child to be so disruptive that he had to leave the classroom. One teacher did recall a student who had behaviour difficulty because of problems in the home.

Other problems they claimed to have eradicated were cases arising from malnutrition, unemployment and . . . thanks in part to an organised movement against it . . . opium addiction. We have no cases of that now, they said. Also no alcoholism because such great changes have taken place in the spirit, habits, customs, and the world outlook of the people. These physicians also noted that problems with the elderly were minimal, and they saw few cases of senile psychosis. 'In our society, they said, old people can live useful lives.'

Before I am accused of being a Communist sympathiser, let me hasten to acknowledge the liabilities of that totalitarian system. The Chinese people are denied fundamental freedoms, which we take for granted in America, and I certainly must oppose a government which forbids its citizens to travel freely, join a labour union, select its own leaders, operate a free press, serve the God of their choice, and so forth. Furthermore, it is likely that the glowing report Dr. Lowinger obtained from Chinese doctors was significantly influenced by their patriotism and revolutionary zeal. On the other hand, we can learn from China's success, and I definitely feel that we Americans would do well to teach our children the virtues of cooperation and respect for the human family. That is, after all, the heart and soul of the Christian message.

Strategy No. 12

DEFUSE THE BOMB OF INFERIORITY

This final suggestion involves an expansion of an idea mentioned briefly in Strategy No. 9, entitled Prepare for Adolescence. I stated at that point, 'There is no greater service that a parent can perform for his preteenager than to "defuse" the self-worth crisis before it arrives, making it appear universal and temporary' *see* page 138. I was referring to the need for a pre-adolescent instructional session that would permit the parent to explain some of the problems and concerns that were likely to develop during the following few years. I now believe that instructional effort should begin at least six years earlier.

In a sense, all of childhood is a preparation for adolescence and beyond. Mothers and fathers are granted a single decade to lay a foundation of values and attitudes that will help their children cope with the future pressures and problems of adulthood. As such, we would all do well to acquaint our young children with the meaning of self-worth and its preservation, since every human being has to deal with that issue at some point in the life cycle.

This teaching process should begin during the kindergarten years, if not before. For example, when your child meets someone who is too shy to speak or even look at him, you might say, 'Why do you suppose Billie is too embarrassed to tell you what he is feeling? Do you think he doesn't have much self-confidence?' (Use the word *confidence* frequently, referring to a kind of courage and belief in one's self.) When your child participates in a school or church programme, compliment him for having the confidence to stand in front of a group without hanging his head or thrusting his tongue in his cheek.

Then as the elementary years unfold, begin focusing on the negative side of that important ingredient. Talk openly about feelings of inferiority and what they mean. For example, 'Did you notice how David acted so silly in class this morning? He was trying hard to make everyone pay attention to him, wasn't he? Do you have any idea why he needs to be noticed every minute of the day? Maybe it's because David doesn't like himself very much. I think he is trying to force people to like him because he thinks he is disrespected. Why don't you try to make friends with David and help him feel better about himself? Would you like to invite him to spend the night?'

Not only will you help your child 'tune in' to the feelings of others through this instruction, but you will also be teaching him to understand his *own* feelings of inadequacy. Each year that passes should bring more explicit understandings about the crisis in worth which comes to everyone. It would be wise to give him an illustration of people who have overcome great feelings of inferiority (such as Eleanor Roosevelt), and ultimately, the *best* examples will come from the struggles of your own adolescent experiences. The goal is to send your pubescent son or daughter into the teen years, armed with four specific concepts: (1) all adolescents go through a time when they don't like themselves very much; (2) most feel ugly and dumb and unliked by their peer group; (3) the worst of this self-doubt will not last very long, although most human beings have to deal with those feelings off and on throughout life; (4) each of us possesses incredible value because we are children of the Creator, who has a specific plan for our lives.

I suppose this twelfth strategy appeals to me not only for its possible contribution to a healthy adolescence, but because it takes us in the direction of human understanding. And how badly that comprehension is needed! I read recently that 80 per cent of the people who get fired from their jobs have not failed to perform as required. In other words, they do not lack *technical* skill or abilities. Their dismissal occurs because *they can't get along with people*. They misunderstand the motives of others and respond with belligerence or insubordination. We can minimise that possibility by training our children to 'see' others in a truer light, while preserving their own dignity and sense of worth.

A FINAL COMMENT

I hope I will not give the reader whiplash by changing direction too quickly, but we must not conclude this revised edition of *How to Build Confidence in Your Child* without considering the biblical concept of 'pride', a how it relates to self-esteem It is my opinion that great confusion has prevailed on this matter among followers of Christ. Some people actually believe that Christians should maintain an attitude of inferiority in order to avoid the pitfalls of self-sufficiency and haughtiness. I don't believe it.

After speaking to a sizeable audience in Boston a few years ago, I was approached by an elderly lady who questioned my views. I had discussed the importance of self-confidence in children, and my comments had contradicted her theology.

She said, 'God wants me to think of myself as being no better than a worm' (referring I suppose, to David's analogy in Psalms 22:6).

'I would like to respect myself,' she continued, 'but God could not approve of that kind of pride, could He?'

I was touched as this sincere little lady spoke. She told me she had been a missionary for forty years, even refusing to marry in order to serve God more completely. While on a foreign field, she had become ill with an exotic disease which now reduced her frail body to ninety-five pounds. As she spoke, I could sense the great love of the Heavenly Father for his faithful servant. She had literally given her life in His work, yet she did not even feel entitled to reflect on a job well done during her closing years on earth.

Unfortunately, this fragile missionary (and thousands of other Christians) had been taught that she was worthless. But that teaching did not come from the Scriptures. Jesus did not leave His throne in heaven to die for the 'worms' of the world. His sacrifice was intended for that little woman, and for me and all of His followers, whom He is not embarrassed to call brothers. What a concept! If Jesus is now my brother, then that puts me in the family of God, and guarantees that I will outlive the universe itself. And that, friends, is what I call genuine self-esteem!

It's true that the Bible clearly condemns the concept of human pride. In fact, God apparently holds a special hatred for this particular sin. I have counted 112 references in the Scripture which specifically warn against an attitude of pride. Proverbs 6:16–19 makes it unmistakably clear:

These six things doth the Lord hate: yea, seven are an abomination unto him: A proud look, a lying tongue, and hands that shed innocent blood, An heart that deviseth wicked imaginations, feet that be swift in running to mischief, A false witness that speaketh lies, and he that soweth discord among brethren.

KING JAMES VERSION

Isn't it interesting that *a proud look* (or *haughtiness*, as paraphrased in the Living Bible) is listed *first* among God's seven most despised sins, apparently outranking adultery, profanity, and other acts of disobedience? Anything given that prominence in the Word had better be avoided scrupulously by those wishing to please the Lord. But first we must interpret the meaning of the word *pride*.

Language is dynamic and the meaning of words changes with the passage of time. And in this instance, the word *pride* has many connotations today which are different from the biblical usage of the word. For example, a parent feels 'pride' when his son or daughter succeeds in school or wins a race. But I can't believe the Lord would be displeased by a father glowing with affection when he thinks of the boy or girl entrusted to his care.

We speak, also, about the 'Pride of the Yankees', or a person taking pride in his work, or the pride of a southern cook. These are very positive emotions that mean the individual is dedicated to his craft, that he has self-confidence, and that he will deliver what he promises. Certainly those attitudes could not represent the pinnacle of the seven deadliest sins.

I'm equally convinced that the Bible does not condemn an attitude of quiet self-respect and dignity. Jesus commanded us to love our neighbours *as* ourselves, implying not only that we are permitted a reasonable expression of self-love, but that love for others is impossible — until we experience a measure of self-respect.

Then what *is* the biblical meaning of pride? I believe sinful pride occurs when our arrogant self-sufficiency leads us to violate the two most basic commandments of Jesus: first, to love God with all our heart, mind and strength; and second, to love our neighbour as ourselves. A proud person is too pompous and haughty to bow humbly before his Maker, confessing his sins and submitting himself to a life of service to God; or he is hateful to his fellowman, disregarding the feelings and needs of others. And as such, most of the ills of the world, including war and crime, can be laid at its door. That's why the writer of Proverbs put 'a proud look' above all other evils, for that is where it belongs.

May I stress, further, that the quest for self-esteem *can* take us in the direction of unacceptable pride. During the past five years, for example, we've seen the rise of the Me generation, nurtured carefully by humanistic psychologists, who accept no scriptural dictates. One of the best-selling books of this era is entitled *Looking Out for No. 1*, which instructs its readers to grab the best for themselves. Widely quoted mottos reflect the same selfish orientation, including IF IT FEELS GOOD, DO IT! and DO YOUR OWN THING. This philosophy of 'me first' has the power to blow our world to pieces, whether applied to marriage, business, or international politics.

For some reason, the Me generation has made its un-official headquarters in the state of California, where I live. Perhaps that's why I appreciate the California jokes which are currently in vogue. For instance, 'How many Cali-fornians does it take to screw in a light bulb? *Answer:* five: one to do the work and four to share the experience.' In reality, however, it's no laughing matter. Followers of the self-seeking philosophy have the highest suicide rate, the highest divorce rate, and the highest incidence of neuroticism in the country. Their experience recalls Jesus's words, 'For anyone wo keeps his life for himself shall lose it; and anyone who loses his life for me shall find it again' (*see* Luke 9:24).

In summary, let me state what I hope has been obvious to this point. *How to Build Confidence in Your Child* does not reflect the philosophy of Me-ism. I have not suggested that children be taught arrogance and self-sufficiency or that they be lured into selfishness. (That will occur without any encouragement from parents.) My purpose has been to help mothers and fathers preserve an inner physical and mental and spiritual health. And I hope this final segment has taken us a few steps further in that direction.

God loves you and your children. So do I.

JAMES C. DOBSON

JOURNEY THROUGH SINGLE PARENTING

A Guide to Finding Fulfilment

Jill Worth

Almost every single parent has become one through crisis, whether they are divorced, widowed or have never married. Only a tiny minority choose to have and raise a child on their own. It is a tough journey to travel.

This book aims to be a travel companion to parents on the journey through single parenting, whether they are just starting out or are a long way down the road. Through true stories and helpful advice, it covers subjects such as loss, anger, loneliness, money, time, sexuality and remarriage. It explores the emotional and practical stages encountered in single parenting and, most importantly, possible ways to finding fulfilment.

JILL WORTH is Editor of *Parentwise* magazine.

ISBN 0 340 65190 3

FINANCIAL TIPS FOR THE FAMILY

An Essential Guide

Keith Tondeur

Money management is a problem and pressure which every family has to face. Keith Tondeur tackles the difficult task with this easy-to-understand guide to family finance, clearly showing how to budget and, if necessary, how to sort out debt.

Written with the aid of practical examples and illustrative case studies, subjects addressed include: maximising income, reducing expenditure and making money go further; encouraging children to handle money responsibly; providing for your retirement; coping financially with redundancy; and handling money pressures. This book seeks to bring financial peace of mind to all families.

KEITH TONDEUR trained as an accountant, worked as a stockbroker for over 20 years and is Director of Credit Action. He is the author of a number of books.

ISBN 0 340 68673 1

HOW TO SUCCEED AS A PARENT

Survival Tips for Busy Mums & Dads

Steve Chalke

Did you notice when your child was born that the instruction manual was missing? Parents today, especially single parents, are frequently out there on their own. And the clock is ticking . . . Valuable parenting time is running out. Steve Chalke shares some of the many insights he's gained from parent-hood in this easy-to-read, practical guide to a hazardous but rewarding task.

Subjects covered include: what is a parent's job description?; how to say sorry for your mistakes; how to avoid lecturing a 2-year-old or talking down to a 12-year-old; how to punish crimes, not mistakes; how to get the most from your child's education; and how and when to tell your child about the 'facts of life'.

STEVE CHALKE is Director of the Oasis Trust, a popular speaker and television presenter, and father of four.

ISBN 0 340 67903 4

THE SPECIAL YEARS

An Essential Guide for Parents of Under Fives

Celia Bowring

Parenthood is an exciting but daunting experience. Humour, encouragement and hope are offered by Celia Bowring in this down-to-earth and practical guide for parents with under five-year-olds, as well as for those planning to become parents in the future.

The book takes mothers and fathers through pregnancy and birth to the early years of childhood, covering topics such as: preparing for parenthood, coping with crying, maintaining discipline, dealing with squabbling siblings and learning to let go. It stresses the crucial importance of the first five years of a child's life, and the value of love, stability and celebrating life to the full.

CELIA BOWRING is Consulting Editor for *Parentwise* magazine, a qualified teacher and mother of three.

ISBN 0 340 68672 3